FREE DVD FREE FREE DVD

From Stress to Success DVD from Trivium Test Prep

Dear Customer,

Thank you for purchasing from Trivium Test Prep! Whether you're looking to join the military, get into college, or advance your career, we're honored to be a part of your journey.

To show our appreciation (and to help you relieve a little of that test-prep stress), we're offering a **FREE *From Stress to Success* DVD** by Trivium Test Prep. Our DVD includes 35 test preparation strategies that will help keep you calm and collected before and during your big exam. All we ask is that you email us your feedback and describe your experience with our product. Amazing, awful, or just so-so: we want to hear what you have to say!

To receive your **FREE *From Stress to Success* DVD**, please email us at 5star@triviumtestprep.com. Include "Free 5 Star" in the subject line and the following information in your email:

1. The title of the product you purchased.
2. Your rating from 1 – 5 (with 5 being the best).
3. Your feedback about the product, including how our materials helped you meet your goals and ways in which we can improve our products.
4. Your full name and shipping address so we can send your **FREE *From Stress to Success* DVD**.

If you have any questions or concerns, please feel free to contact me directly.

Thank you, and good luck with your studies!

Alyssa Wagoner
Quality Control
alyssa.wagoner@triviumtestprep.com

Checked for writing	Staff Initials	Date

TASC Practice Tests
350 TEST PREP QUESTIONS FOR THE
TEST ASSESSING SECONDARY COMPLETION EXAM

TABLE OF CONTENTS

INTRODUCTION   i

1 MATHEMATICS   1

    Answer Key   15

2 READING   25

    Answer Key   51

3 SCIENCE   57

    Answer Key   65

4 WRITING   67

    Answer Key   77

5 SOCIAL STUDIES   81

    Answer Key   99

INTRODUCTION

Congratulations on choosing to take the TASC! By purchasing this book, you've taken the first step toward getting your high-school equivalency, which will greatly expand your career options.

This guide will provide you with a detailed overview of the TASC so you know exactly what to expect on test day. We'll take you through all the concepts covered on the test and give you the opportunity to test your knowledge with practice questions. Even if it's been awhile since you last took a major test, don't worry; we'll make sure you're more than ready!

WHAT IS THE TASC

The Test Assessing Secondary Completion, or TASC, is a high school equivalency assessment. It measures whether test takers have a high-school-level understanding of five basic subjects: reading, writing, mathematics, social studies, and science. In short, it tests everything taught in high school, so that if you didn't earn a diploma, you can still prove you have the equivalent knowledge.

WHAT IS ON THE TASC?

The TASC test assesses your proficiency in high-school-level subject areas using multiple-choice, grid-in, and essay questions. You must pass each subtest in order to receive high school equivalency. Constructed-response questions are short open-ended questions that help scorers of your test to measure your skills in a way that cannot be determined by simple multiple-choice questions. There is only one open-ended question in each subtest of the TASC. When you take the computerized test, you will be expected to answer one technology-enhanced question on each subtest. This question is similar to multiple-choice questions, and may require that you drag and drop answer choices in order to select the correct answer or type to answer a question.

As a part of the writing subtest, you will need to answer one essay question. You will be tasked with writing either an informational or argumentative essay in response to a provided prompt and reading passage(s); the prompt will indicate if you are to write an informational or argumentative essay. The reading passage(s) supplements the prompt with the information necessary to construct your essay. Regardless of whether you are responding to an argumentative or informational essay prompt, the writing should discuss a clear topic and support it with relevant evidence from the provided text(s). The essay is scored by two graders who will assign a score of a number between 0 – 4 based on the answer's adherence to the TASC scoring rubric. A score of a 4 is earned by a response that is well developed and incorporates relevant textual evidence. A complete essay that examines the prompt can earn a score of a 3, while a score of a 2 will be given to an answer that is oversimplified or incomplete. A response that serves as an attempt to examine the prompt will earn a 1, and a score of a 0 will be given to an irrelevant or incorrect response.

What's on the TASC?

SUBTEST	TOTAL NUMBER OF QUESTIONS	TIME	SECTIONS	PERCENTAGE
Mathematics	42 or 43 multiple-choice		Numbers and quantity	13%
	11 gridded-response		Algebra	26%
	1 constructed-response	50 minutes	Functions	26%
	1 computer-based item		Geometry	23%
	No calculator questions	55 minutes	Statistics	12%
Writing	50 or 51 multiple-choice		Writing	15%
	1 constructed-response		Grammar/usage	30%
	1 computer-based item	105 minutes	Capitalization/ punctuation/spelling	25%
	1 writing prompt		Knowledge of language	30%
Reading	48 or 49 multiple-choice		Informational texts	70%
	1 constructed-response	75 minutes		
	1 computer-based item		Literary texts	30%
Science	48 or 49 multiple-choice		Physical sciences	36%
	1 constructed-response	85 minutes	Life sciences	36%
	1 computer-based item		Earth/space sciences	28%
Social Studies	48 or 49 multiple-choice		U.S. history	25%
	1 constructed-response		World history	15%
	1 computer-based item	75 minutes	Civics/government	25%
	8 stimuli		Geography	15%
			Economics	20%

Note that times assigned for Spanish tests are five minutes longer in each category.

HOW IS THE TASC SCORED?

On the TASC, each subtest is scored separately. There is no penalty for guessing on TASC tests, so be sure to eliminate answer choices and answer every question. If you still do not know the answer, guess; you may get it right! The number of correctly answered questions counts as 1 point, and then scores are scaled to a number in the range 300-800, a passing score being 500. The essay is scored a number from 0 – 4 and then doubled to create your scaled score from 0 – 8. To pass the writing subtest of the TASC, you need a score of at least 500 on the multiple-choice and a 2 on the writing section. You must pass each subtest to pass the overall test. Please note that individual states may have different requirements for earning high school equivalency, so be sure to check your state's score requirements.

Scores are reported up to ten days after your testing date. You can access your score on your online account. Score reports contain the overall scaled score, the passing status, and indices that pinpoint your performance on each content area of the test. You can use the indices to better understand your strengths and weaknesses in the material.

How is the TASC administered?

This test is administered as a paper-and-pencil test or as a computerized test. You are encouraged to take the version of the test that is most comfortable for you. There is no difference in difficulty between the two versions; both have the same time limit and cover the same content. The online test will have one less multiple-choice question that is replaced with a technology-enhanced question that may require that you drag and drop answer choices to select the correct answer or type to answer a question. The TASC website allows you to take a practice test to acclimate yourself to the computerized format if you choose to take this version. Be sure to check with your testing facility to see if they offer the version of the test that you'd like to take.

The TASC is administered at private testing facilities across the nation. (You can find a list of these locations at www.tasctest.com.) Each location may administer the exam slightly differently, so ask at your particular location about the details of test administration. You'll want to ask when the test begins, when breaks are offered, and what kind of materials you're allowed to bring with you to the test.

About Trivium Test Prep

Trivium Test Prep uses industry professionals with decades' worth of knowledge in their fields, proven with degrees and honors in law, medicine, business, education, the military, and more, to produce high-quality test prep books for students.

Our study guides are specifically designed to increase any student's score, regardless of his or her current skill level. Our books are also shorter and more concise than typical study guides, so you can increase your score while significantly decreasing your study time.

How to Use This Guide

Because we have eliminated "filler" or "fluff," you'll be able to work through the guide at a significantly faster pace than you would with other test prep books. By allowing you to focus only on those concepts that will increase your score, we'll make your study time shorter and more effective.

Now that you have a firm understanding of the exam, don't forget that learning how to study, as well as how to successfully pass an exam, is just as important as the content. Trivium Test Prep would like to remind you as you begin your studies that we are offering a **FREE** *From Stress to Success* **DVD**. Our DVD includes 35 test preparation strategies that will help keep you calm and collected before and during your big exam. All we ask is that you email us your feedback and describe your experience with our product. Amazing, awful, or just so-so: we want to hear what you have to say!

To receive your **FREE** *From Stress to Success* DVD, please email us at 5star@triviumtestprep.com. Include

"Free 5 Star" in the subject line and the following information in your email:

1. The title of the product you purchased.
2. Your rating from 1 – 5 (with 5 being the best).
3. Your feedback about the product, including how our materials helped you meet your goals and ways in which we can improve our products.
4. Your full name and shipping address so we can send your **FREE** *From Stress to Success* **DVD**.

We hope you find the rest of this study guide helpful.

TEST YOUR KNOWLEDGE

MATHEMATICS

Directions: Read the problem carefully, and choose the best answer.

1. A car dealership's commercials claim that this year's models are 20% off the list price, plus they will pay the first 3 monthly payments. If a car is listed for $26,580, and the monthly payments are set at $250, which of the following is the total potential savings?

   A) $1,282

   B) $5,566

   C) $6,066

   D) $20,514

2. A dry cleaner charges $3 per shirt, $6 per pair of pants, and an extra $5 per item for mending. Annie drops off 5 shirts and 4 pairs of pants, 2 of which need mending. Assuming the cleaner charges an 8% sales tax, which of the following will be the amount of Annie's total bill?

   A) $45.08

   B) $49.00

   C) $52.92

   D) $88.20

3. A sandwich shop earns $4 for every sandwich ($s$) it sells, $2 for every drink ($d$), and $1 for every cookie ($c$). If this is all the shop sells, which of the following equations represents what the shop's revenue (r) is over three days?

   A) $r = 4s + 2d + 1c$

   B) $r = 8s + 4d + 2c$

   C) $r = 12s + 6d + 3c$

   D) $r = 16s + 8d + 4c$

4. Which of the following is the y-intercept of the line whose equation is $7y - 42x + 7 = 0$?

   A) $\left(\frac{1}{6}, 0\right)$

   B) $(6, 0)$

   C) $(0, -1)$

   D) $(-1, 0)$

5. $4 - \frac{1}{2^2} + 24 \div (8 + 12)$

   Simplify the expression. Which of the following is correct?

   A) 1.39

   B) 2.74

   C) 4.95

   D) 15.28

6. A rectangular field has area of 1452 square feet. If the width is three times greater than the length, which of the following is the length of the field?

A) 22 feet

B) 44 feet

C) 242 feet

D) 1452 feet

7. The owner of a newspaper has noticed that print subscriptions have gone down 40% while online subscriptions have gone up 60%. Print subscriptions once accounted for 70% of the newspaper's business, and online subscriptions accounted for 25%. Which of the following is the overall percentage growth or decline in business?

A) 13% decline

B) 15% decline

C) 28% growth

D) Business has stayed the same.

8. $(6.4)(2.8) \div 0.4$

Simplify the expression. Which of the following is correct?

A) 16.62

B) 17.92

C) 41.55

D) 44.80

9. Bridget is repainting her rectangular bedroom. Two walls measure 15 feet by 9 feet, and the other two measure 12.5 feet by 9 feet. One gallon of paint covers an average of 32 square meters. Which of the following is the number of gallons of paint that Bridget will use? (There are 3.28 feet in 1 meter.)

A) 0.72 gallons

B) 1.43 gallons

C) 4.72 gallons

D) 15.5 gallons

10. $5\frac{2}{3} \times 1\frac{7}{8} \div \frac{1}{3}$

Simplify the expression. Which of the following is correct?

A. $3\frac{13}{24}$

B. $6\frac{3}{4}$

C. $15\frac{3}{4}$

D. $31\frac{7}{8}$

11. Based on a favorable performance review at work, Matt receives a $\frac{3}{20}$ increase in his hourly wage. If his original hourly wage is represented by w, which of the following represents his new wage?

A) $0.15w$

B) $0.85w$

C) $1.12w$

D) $1.15w$

12. A restaurant employs servers, hosts, and managers in a ratio of 9:2:1. If there are 36 total employees, which of the following is the number of hosts at the restaurant?

A) 3

B) 4

C) 6

D) 8

13. If x is the proportion of men who play an instrument, y is the proportion of women who play an instrument, and z is the total number of men, which of the following is true?

A. $\frac{z}{x}$ = number of men who play an instrument

B. $(1 - z)x$ = number of men who do not play an instrument

C. $(1 - x)z$ = number of men who do not play an instrument

D. $(1 - y)z$ = number of women who do not play an instrument

14. A woman's dinner bill comes to $48.30. If she adds a 20% tip, which of the following will be her total bill?

A) $9.66

B) $38.64

C) $48.30

D) $57.96

15. Which of the following lists is in order from least to greatest?

A) $\frac{1}{7}$, 0.125, $\frac{6}{9}$, 0.60

B) $\frac{1}{7}$, 0.125, 0.60, $\frac{6}{9}$

C) 0.125, $\frac{1}{7}$, 0.60, $\frac{6}{9}$

D) 0.125, $\frac{1}{7}$, 0.125, $\frac{6}{9}$, 0.60

16. Which of the following is equivalent to 3.28?

A) $3\frac{1}{50}$

B) $3\frac{1}{25}$

C) $3\frac{7}{50}$

D) $3\frac{7}{25}$

17. $x \div 7 = x - 36$

Solve the equation. Which of the following is correct?

A) $x = 6$

B) $x = 42$

C) $x = 126$

D) $x = 252$

18. After taxes, a worker earned $15,036 in 7 months. Which of the following is the amount the worker earned in 2 months?

A) $2,148

B) $4,296

C) $6,444

D) $8,592

19. If m represents a car's average mileage in miles per gallon, p represents the price of gas in dollars per gallon, and d represents a distance in miles, which of the following algebraic equations represents the cost c of gas per mile?

A) $c = \frac{dp}{m}$

B) $c = \frac{p}{m}$

C) $c = \frac{mp}{d}$

D) $c = \frac{m}{p}$

20. Melissa is ordering fencing to enclose a square area of 5625 square feet. Which of the following is the number of feet of fencing she needs?

A) 75 feet

B) 150 feet

C) 300 feet

D) 5,625 feet

21. Adam is painting the outside of a 4-walled shed. The shed is 5 feet wide, 4 feet deep, and 7 feet high. Which of the following is the amount of paint Adam will need for the four walls?

A) 80 ft.²

B) 126 ft.²

C) 140 ft.²

D) 560 ft.²

22. A circular swimming pool has a circumference of 49 feet. Which of the following is the diameter of the pool?

A) 15.6 feet

B) 17.8 feet

C) 49 feet

D) 153.9 feet

CONTINUE

23. Table 1.1. Employee Hours

EMPLOYEE	HOURS WORKED
Suzanne	42
Joe	38
Mark	25
Ellen	50
Jill	45
Rob	46
Nicole	17
Deb	41

The table above shows the number of hours worked by employees during the week. Which of the following is the median number of hours worked per week by the employees?

A) 38

B) 41

C) 42

D) 41.5

24. According to the graph, which of the following was Sam's average monthly income from January through May? (Round to the nearest hundred.)

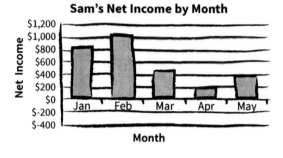

Sam's Net Income by Month

A) $200

B) $500

C) $600

D) $1,100

25. Which of the following is equivalent to 8 pounds and 8 ounces? (Round to the nearest tenth of a kilogram.)

A) 3.6 kilograms

B) 3.9 kilograms

C) 17.6 kilograms

D) 18.7 kilograms

26. $(4.71 \times 10^3) - (2.98 \times 10^2)$

Simplify the expression. Which of the following is correct?

A) 1.73×10

B) 4.412×10^2

C) 1.73×10^3

D) 4.412×10^3

27. Which of the following is not a negative value?

A) $(-3)(-1)(2)(-1)$

B) $14 - 7 + (-7)$

C) $7 - 10 + (-8)$

D) $-5(-2)(-3)$

28. $10^2 - 7(3 - 4) - 25$

Simplify the expression. Which of the following is correct?

A) -12

B) 2

C) 68

D) 82

29. $\dfrac{5^2(3) + 3(-2)^2}{4 + 3^2 - 2(5 - 8)}$

Simplify the expression. Which of the following is correct?

A) $\dfrac{9}{8}$

B) $\dfrac{87}{19}$

C) 9

D) $\dfrac{21}{2}$

30. Anna is buying fruit at the farmers' market. She selects 1.2 kilograms of apples, 800 grams of bananas, and 300 grams of strawberries. The farmer charges her a flat rate of $4 per kilogram. Which of the following is the total cost of her produce?

A) $4.40

B) $5.24

C) $9.20

D) $48.80

31. $\left(1\frac{1}{2}\right)\left(2\frac{2}{3}\right) \div 1\frac{1}{4}$

Simplify the expression. Which of the following is correct?

A) $3\frac{1}{12}$

B) $3\frac{1}{5}$

C) 4

D) 5

32. Which of the following lists is in order from least to greatest?

A) $2^{-1}, -\frac{4}{3}, (-1)^3, \frac{2}{5}$

B) $-\frac{4}{3}, (-1)^3, 2^{-1}, \frac{2}{5}$

C) $-\frac{4}{3}, \frac{2}{5}, 2^{-1}, (-1)^3$

D) $-\frac{4}{3}, (-1)^3, \frac{2}{5}, 2^{-1}$

33. Which of the following is 2.7834 rounded to the nearest tenth?

A) 2.7

B) 2.78

C) 2.8

D) 2.88

34. $\frac{4x-5}{3} = \frac{\frac{1}{2}(2x-6)}{5}$

Simplify the expression. Which of the following is the value of x?

A) $-\frac{2}{7}$

B) $-\frac{4}{17}$

C) $\frac{16}{17}$

D) $\frac{8}{7}$

35. $8x - 6 = 3x + 24$

Solve the equation. Which of the following is correct?

A) $x = 2.5$

B) $x = 3.6$

C) $x = 5$

D) $x = 6$

36. A student gets 42 questions out of 48 correct on a quiz. Which of the following is the percentage of questions that the student answered correctly?

A) 1.14%

B) 82.50%

C) 85.00%

D) 87.50%

37. $4x \div (x - 1)$

Which of the following is the value of the expression above when $x = 5$?

A) 0

B) 1

C) 4

D) 5

38. Which of the following is the slope of the graph below?

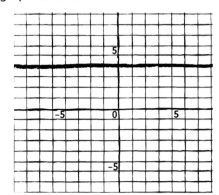

A) ∞

B) non-existent

C) 0

D) 1

CONTINUE

39. Alex, David, and Rachel go out to dinner. Alex and David decide to split an appetizer that costs $8.50, and Rachel gets her own appetizer that costs $6.50. Rachel orders lemonade that costs $3, while Alex and David drink the free water. They all order entrées that cost the same price. They split up the bill according to what each person ordered. Which of the following states how much less Alex and David will pay than Rachel?

A) $1.00

B) $5.00

C) $5.25

D) $7.25

40. There are 450 students in the tenth grade. Of these, 46% are boys. If 21% of the girls have already turned 16, which of the following is the number of girls in the tenth grade who are 16?

A) 43

B) 51

C) 54

D) 94

41. A faucet is leaking 1 drop every 4 seconds. If 1 gallon is equal to 15,140 drops, which of the following lengths of time will it take for this faucet to leak 1 gallon of water?

A) 1 hour, 3 minutes, 5 seconds

B) 4 hours, 12 minutes, 20 seconds

C) 16 hours, 49 minutes, 20 seconds

D) 18 hours, 24 minutes, 5 seconds

42. $(3 + 5)^2 + 24 \div 16 - 5 \div 2$

Simplify the expression. Which of the following is correct?

A) 0.25

B) 30.25

C) 33

D) 63

43. Ashley has been training for a 10-kilometer race. Her average training pace is 8 minutes and 15 seconds per mile. If she maintains this pace during the race, which of the following will be her finishing time? (1 mile = 5280 feet; 1 foot = 0.3048 meters)

A) 51:23

B) 50:53

C) 51:14

D) 82:30

44. $\frac{8}{15} \div \frac{1}{6}$

Simplify the expression. Which of the following is correct?

A) $3\frac{1}{15}$

B) $\frac{15}{48}$

C) $\frac{4}{45}$

D) $3\frac{1}{5}$

45. A marinade recipe calls for 2 tablespoons of lemon juice for $\frac{1}{4}$ cup of olive oil. Which of the following is the amount of lemon juice that should be used with $\frac{2}{3}$ cup olive oil?

A) $5\frac{1}{3}$ tbsp.

B) $\frac{3}{4}$ tbsp.

C) 4 tbsp.

D) $2\frac{1}{3}$ tbsp.

46. If x represents the proportion of ninth graders in a particular school who are female, and y represents the proportion of students in the school who are ninth graders, which of the following is the expression for the proportion of students in the school who are female ninth graders?

A) $x + y$

B) $\frac{x}{y}$

C) xy

D) $\frac{y}{x}$

47. Toledo has been working full time but would like to cut back to part time. He normally works from 9:00 a.m. to 5:00 p.m. Monday through Friday. Now he leaves at 1:00 p.m. on Tuesdays and Thursdays. Which of the following is the percentage by which he decreased his weekly work hours?

A) 20%

B) 25%

C) 30%

D) 80%

48. Which of the following lists is in order from least to greatest?

A) $\frac{1}{24} < \frac{3}{32} < \frac{5}{48} < \frac{2}{16} < \frac{3}{16}$

B) $\frac{1}{24} < \frac{5}{48} < \frac{3}{32} < \frac{2}{16} < \frac{3}{16}$

C) $\frac{1}{24} < \frac{3}{32} < \frac{2}{16} < \frac{3}{16} < \frac{5}{48}$

D) $\frac{1}{24} < \frac{2}{16} < \frac{3}{32} < \frac{3}{16} < \frac{5}{48}$

49. $3a + 4 = 2a$

Solve the equation. Which of the following is correct?

A) $a = -4$

B) $a = 4$

C) $a = \frac{-4}{5}$

D) $a = \frac{4}{5}$

50. Caroline reads 40 pages in 45 minutes. Which of the following is the approximate number minutes it will take her to read 265 pages?

A) 202 minutes

B) 236 minutes

C) 265 minutes

D) 298 minutes

51. Jane earns $15 per hour babysitting. If she starts out with $275 in her bank account, which of the following equations represents the amount of hours she will need to spend babysitting in order for her account to reach $400?

A) $275 = 400 + 15h$

B) $400 = 15h$

C) $400 = \frac{15}{h} + 275$

D) $400 = 275 + 15h$

52. Which of the following is the total surface area of a box that is 12 inches long, 18 inches wide, and 6 inches high?

A) 144 sq. in.

B) 396 sq. in.

C) 792 sq. in.

D) 1,296 cu. in.

53. Which of the following has the greatest numeric value?

A) $-4(3)(-2)$

B) $-16 - 17 + 31$

C) $18 - 15 + 27$

D) $-20 + 10 + 10$

54. A pizza has a diameter of 10 inches. If a slice with a central angle of 40 degrees is cut from the pizza, which of the following will be the surface area of the pizza slice?

A) 9.2. sq. in.

B) 8.7 sq. in.

C) 3.5 sq. in.

D) 17.4 sq. in.

55. Meg rolled a 6-sided die 4 times, and her first 3 rolls were 1, 3, and 5. If the average of the 4 rolls is 2.5, which of the following was the value of the 4th roll?

A) 1

B) 2

C) 3

D) 5

56. The data set below shows the number of instruments played by students in the seventh and tenth grades. Which of the following is the difference in the average number of instruments played by seventh- and tenth-graders?

Table 1.2. Instruments Played

STUDENT	GRADE	NUMBER OF INSTRUMENTS
Alison	7	2
Dana	10	0
Jerry	7	1
Sam	7	1
Luke	10	1
Philip	7	2
Briana	10	1
Laura	10	0
Angie	7	2

A) 0.5

B) 1

C) 1.1

D) 2.1

57. If there are 3.28 feet in 1 meter, which of the following is equivalent to 55 meters? (Round to the nearest tenth.)

A) 16.8 feet

B) 21.7 feet

C) 139.7 feet

D) 180.4 feet

58. $-(3)^2 + (5 - 7)^2 - 3(4 - 8)$

Simplify the expression. Which of the following is correct?

A) −17

B) −1

C) 7

D) 25

59. The pie chart below shows a high school graduating class' enrollment in 4 types of universities: small private, large private, small public, and large public. Of the students who enrolled in a public university, which of the following is the percentage enrolled in a small public university?

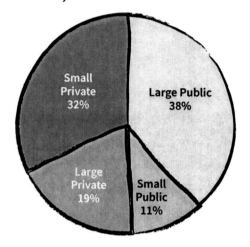

A) 11%

B) 22%

C) 27%

D) 29%

60. $(3^2 \div 1^3) - (4 - 8^2) + 2^4$

Simplify the expression. Which of the following is correct?

A) −35

B) −4

C) 28

D) 85

61. $17.38 - 19.26 + 14.2$

Simplify the expression. Which of the following is correct?

A) 12.08

B) 12.32

C) 16.08

D) 16.22

62. A cylindrical canister is 9 inches high and has a diameter of 5 inches. The formula for the volume of a cylinder is $V = \pi r^2 h$ where r is the radius and h is the height. Which of the following is the volume of the canister?

A) 176.6 in²

B) 45 in²

C) 141.4 in²

D) 706.9 in²

63. $\frac{7}{8} - \frac{1}{10} - \frac{2}{3}$

Simplify the expression. Which of the following is correct?

A) $\frac{1}{30}$

B) $\frac{13}{120}$

C) $\frac{4}{21}$

D) $\frac{4}{105}$

64. Which of the following is equivalent to $4\frac{10}{11}$?

A) 4.09

B) $4.\overline{09}$

C) 4.90

D) $4.\overline{90}$

65. Which of the following shows 74,365 rounded to the nearest hundred and to the nearest thousand?

A) hundred: 74,400; thousand: 74,000

B) hundred: 74,300; thousand: 75,000

C) hundred: 74,400; thousand: 75,000

D) hundred: 74,300; thousand: 74,000

66. A store recorded the following sales over one week:

Table 1.3. Recorded Sales

DAY	SALES
Monday	$300
Tuesday	$250
Wednesday	$550
Thursday	$475
Friday	$325
Saturday	$800

Which of the following is the ratio of the highest amount of sales to total sales for the week and the ratio of lowest amount of sales to total sales for the week?

A) lowest: $\frac{13}{108}$; highest: $\frac{8}{27}$

B) lowest: $\frac{13}{108}$; highest: $\frac{11}{54}$

C) lowest: $\frac{5}{54}$; highest: $\frac{8}{27}$

D) lowest: $\frac{5}{54}$; highest: $\frac{11}{54}$

67. $10y - 8 - 2y = 4y - 22 + 5y$

Solve the equation. Which of the following is correct?

A) $y = -4\frac{2}{3}$

B) $y = 14$

C) $y = 30$

D) $y = -30$

68. Which of the following is equivalent to 37.5%?

A) 0.0375

B) 0.375

C) 3.75

D) 37.5

69. An employee makes $37,500 per year and receives a 5.5% raise. Which of the following is the employee's new salary?

A) $35,437.50

B) $35,625

C) $39,375

D) $39,562.50

70. Which of the following sets of numbers is listed in order from least to greatest?

A) $-0.95, 0, \frac{2}{5}, 0.35, \frac{3}{4}$

B) $-1, -\frac{1}{10}, -0.11, \frac{5}{6}, 0.75$

C) $-\frac{3}{4}, -0.2, 0, \frac{2}{3}, 0.55$

D) $-1.1, -\frac{4}{5}, -0.13, 0.7, \frac{9}{11}$

71. The population of a town was 7250 in 2014 and 7375 in 2015. Which of the following was the percent increase from 2014 to 2015? (Round to the nearest tenth.)

A) 1.5%

B) 1.6%

C) 1.7%

D) 1.8%

72. Which of the following choices places these fractions in the correct order from greatest to least?

$$\frac{1}{3}, -\frac{1}{4}, \frac{1}{2}, -\frac{1}{5}, \frac{1}{7}, -\frac{1}{6}$$

A) $\frac{1}{2}, \frac{1}{3}, \frac{1}{7}, -\frac{1}{5}, -\frac{1}{6}, -\frac{1}{4}$

B) $\frac{1}{2}, \frac{1}{3}, \frac{1}{7}, -\frac{1}{6}, -\frac{1}{5}, -\frac{1}{4}$

C) $\frac{1}{2}, \frac{1}{7}, \frac{1}{3}, -\frac{1}{4}, -\frac{1}{5}, -\frac{1}{6}$

D) $\frac{1}{2}, \frac{1}{3}, \frac{1}{7}, -\frac{1}{6}, -\frac{1}{4}, -\frac{1}{5}$

73. A sporting goods store is offering an additional 30% off all clearance items. Angie purchases a pair of running shoes on clearance for $65.00. If the shoes originally cost $85.00, what was her total discount?

A) 53.5%

B) 46.5%

C) 22.9%

D) 39.2%

74. Which of the following is not a rational number?

A) -4

B) $\frac{1}{5}$

C) $0.8\overline{33}$

D) $\sqrt{2}$

75. What is 1230.932567 rounded to the nearest hundredths place?

A) 1200

B) 1230.9326

C) 1230.93

D) 1230

76. What is the absolute value of -9?

A) -9

B) 9

C) 0

D) -1

77. Add $0.98 + 45.102 + 32.3333 + 31 + 0.00009$.

A) 368.573

B) 210.536299

C) 109.41539

D) 99.9975

78. $(9 \div 3) \times (8 \div 4) =$

A) 1

B) 6

C) 72

D) 576

79. $7.95 \div 1.5 =$

A) 2.4

B) 5.3

C) 6.2

D) 7.3

80. A bag contains twice as many red marbles as blue marbles, and the number of blue marbles is 88% of the number of green marbles. If g represents the number of green marbles, which of the following expressions represents the total number of marbles in the bag?

A) $3.88g$

B) $3.64g$

C) $2.64g$

D) $2.32g$

81. Melissa is ordering fencing to enclose a square area of 5625 square feet. How many feet of fencing does she need?

A) 75

B) 150

C) 300

D) 5,625

82. If a discount of 25% off the retail price of a desk saves Mark $45, what was the desk's original price?

A) $135

B) $160

C) $180

D) $210

83. Adam owns 4 times as many shirts as he has pairs of pants, and he has 5 pairs of pants for every 2 pairs of shoes. What is the ratio of Adam's shirts to Adam's shoes?

A) 25 shirts: 1 pair shoes

B) 10 shirts : 1 pair shoes

C) 20 shirts : 1 pair shoes

D) 15 shirts : 2 pairs shoes

84. Patrick is coming home from vacation in Costa Rica and wants to fill one of his suitcases with bags of Costa Rican coffee. The weight limit for his suitcase is 22 kilograms, and the suitcase itself weighs 3.2 kilograms. If each bag of coffee weighs 800 grams, how many bags can he bring in his suitcase without going over the limit?

A) 2

B) 4

C) 23

D) 27

85. Convert 0.28 into a fraction.

A) $\frac{9}{25}$

B) $\frac{7}{45}$

C) $\frac{7}{25}$

D) $\frac{8}{15}$

ANSWER KEY

1. C)

First calculate 20% of the list price:

$0.20 \times \$26{,}580 = \$5{,}316$

Next calculate the savings over the first 3 months of payments:

$3 \text{ months} \times \$250/\text{month} = \$750$

Find the total savings:

$\$5{,}316 + \$750 = \$6{,}066$

2. C)

First find the total cost before tax:

5 shirts $\times$ \$3/shirt $+$ 4 pants $\times$ \$6/pants $+$ 2 items mended $\times$ \$5/item mended $= \$49$

Now multiply this amount by 1.08 to account for the added 8% sales tax:

$\$49 \times 1.08 = \$52.92$

3. A)

Let s be the number of sandwiches sold. Each sandwich earns \$4, so selling s sandwiches at \$4 each results in revenue of $\$4s$. Similarly, d drinks at \$2 each gives $\$2d$ of income and cookies bring in $\$1c$. Summing these values gives a total of revenue $= 4s + 2d + 1c$.

4. C)

The y-intercept will have an x value of 0. This eliminates choices A), B) and D). Plug $x = 0$ into the equation and solve for y to find the y-intercept:

$7y - 42(0) + 7 = 0$, so $7y = -7$ and therefore $y = -1$. The correct answer is $(0, -1)$, which is answer C).

5. C)

First complete the operations in parentheses:

$4 - \frac{1}{2^2} + 24 \div (8 + 12) = 4 - \frac{1}{2^2} + 24 \div (20)$

Next simplify the exponents:

$4 - \frac{1}{2^2} + 24 \div (20) = 4 - \frac{1}{4} + 24 \div (20)$

Then complete multiplication and division operations: $4 - \frac{1}{4} + 24 \div (20) = 4 - 0.25 + 1.2$

Finally complete addition and subtraction operations: $4 - 0.25 + 1.2 = 4.95$

6. A)

The area of a rectangle is *length* $\times$ *width*, so $A = L(3L)$. The area was given, so $1452 = 3L^2$

Solving for L: $484 = L^2$ and $L = \pm22$.

Since length must be positive, $L = 22$ feet.

7. A)

Calculate the decline:

40% decline in 70% of the business $= 0.40 \times 0.70 = 0.28 = 28\%$ decline

Calculate the growth:

60% growth in 25% of the business $= 0.60 \times 0.25 = 0.15 = 15\%$ growth

Find the net change:

28% decline + 15% growth = $-0.28 + 0.15 =$
$-0.13 = 13\%$ decline

8. D)

The first step is to multiply (resulting in 17.92);
then divide the result by 0.4 (making 44.80 the
solution).

9. B)

First convert the dimensions to meters:

$15 \text{ ft.} \times \dfrac{1 \text{ m}}{3.28 \text{ ft.}} = 4.57 \text{ m}$

$9 \text{ ft.} \times \dfrac{1 \text{ m}}{3.28 \text{ ft.}} = 2.74 \text{ m}$

$12.5 \text{ ft.} \times \dfrac{1 \text{ m}}{3.28 \text{ ft.}} = 3.81 \text{ m}$

Next find the total area in square meters:

total area = $2(4.57 \text{ m} \times 2.74 \text{ m}) + 2(3.81 \text{ m} \times 2.74$
$\text{m}) = 45.9 \text{ m}^2$

Finally convert the area to gallons of paint:

$45.9 \text{ m}^2 \times \dfrac{1 \text{ gallon}}{32 \text{ m}^2} = 1.43 \text{ gallons}$

10. D)

First convert mixed fractions to improper
fractions:

$5\frac{2}{3} \times 1\frac{7}{8} \div \frac{1}{3} = \frac{17}{3} \times \frac{15}{8} \div \frac{1}{3}$

Next flip the divisor fraction and multiply:

$\frac{17}{3} \times \frac{15}{8} \div \frac{1}{3} = \frac{17}{3} \times \frac{15}{8} \times \frac{3}{1} =$
$\frac{17 \times 15 \times 3}{3 \times 8 \times 1} = \frac{765}{24}$

Now divide the numerator by the denominator
to convert back to a mixed fraction:

$\frac{765}{24} = 31\frac{21}{24}$

Finally find the greatest common factor to
reduce the fraction:

$31\frac{21}{24} = 31\frac{21 \div 3}{24 \div 3} = 31\frac{7}{8}$

11. D)

A $\frac{3}{20}$ increase means the new wage is
$w + w\left(\frac{3}{20}\right)$, or $w\left(1 + \frac{3}{20}\right)$.

Convert the fraction to decimal form:

$\frac{3}{20} = \frac{3}{20}\left(\frac{5}{5}\right) = \frac{15}{100} = 0.15$

The new wage is:

$w(1 + 0.15) = 1.15w$

12. C)

In algebraic terms, the ratio can be expressed
with the following equation:

$9x + 2x + 1x = 36$

Here, x represents some common factor by
which each number of employees was divided
to reduce the ratio. Solve for x, then find $2x$ to
solve for the number of hosts:

$9x + 2x + 1x = 36$

$12x = 36$

$x = 3$

$2x = 2 \times 3 = 6$

13. C)

$(1 - x)$ = proportion of men who do not play an
instrument

$(1 - x) = \dfrac{\text{number of men who do not play an instrument}}{z}$

$(1 - x)z$ = number of men who do not play an
instrument

14. D)

Adding 20% is equivalent to paying 120% of the
bill:

$\$48.30 \times \dfrac{120}{100} = \$57.96$

15. C)

Convert the fractions to decimals:

$\frac{6}{9} \approx 0.67$

$\frac{1}{7} \approx 0.14$

Now order the numbers from smallest to
largest:

$0.125 < 0.14 < 0.60 < 0.67$

16. D)

Because the last decimal digit is in the
hundredths place, the decimal part of the
number is written as a fraction over 100. The
fraction of $\frac{28}{100}$ reduces to $\frac{7}{25}$.

17. B)

Start by multiplying both sides by 7:

$7(x \div 7) = 7(x - 36)$

$x = 7x - 252$

Now subtract $7x$ from both sides:

$x - 7x = 7x - 252 - 7x$

$-6x = -252$

Finally divide both sides by -6:

$\frac{-6x}{-6} = \frac{-252}{-6}$

$x = 42$

18. B)

A proportion is written using two ratios relating amount earned to months, with x representing the unknown amount:

$\frac{15,036}{7} = \frac{x}{2}$.

The proportion is solved by cross-multiplying and dividing: $7x = 30,072$, $x = 4,296$. The solution is $4,296.

19. B)

The cost c of gas has units dollars per mile. Construct an expression that yields these units:

$\frac{p}{m} = \frac{\left(\frac{\$}{\text{gal.}}\right)}{\left(\frac{\text{mi.}}{\text{gal.}}\right)} = \frac{(\$)(\cancel{\text{gal.}})}{(\text{mi.})(\cancel{\text{gal.}})} = \frac{\$}{\text{mi.}}$

20. C)

Use the area to find the length of one side of the square:

$A = l \times w = l^2$

$5,625 \text{ ft.}^2 = l^2$

$l = \sqrt{5,625 \text{ ft.}^2} = 75 \text{ ft.}$

Now multiply the side length by 4 to find the perimeter:

$P = 4l$

$P = 4(75 \text{ ft.}) = 300 \text{ ft.}$

21. B)

Find the area of all of the sides of the shed. Two walls measure 5 feet by 7 feet; the other two walls measure 4 feet by 7 feet:

$A = 2l_1w_1 + 2l_2w_2$

$A = 2(5 \text{ ft.})(7 \text{ ft.}) + 2(4 \text{ ft.})(7 \text{ ft.})$

$A = 70 \text{ ft.}^2 + 56 \text{ ft.}^2 = 126 \text{ ft.}^2$

22. A)

The formula for the circumference of a circle is:

$C = 2\pi r$

Because $d = 2r$, this formula can be rewritten:

$C = \pi d$

$49 \text{ ft.} = \pi d$

$d = \frac{49 \text{ ft.}}{\pi} = 15.6 \text{ ft.}$

23. D)

To find the median, first order the data points from smallest to largest:

17, 25, 38, 41, 42, 45, 46, 50

There is an even number of data points. Locate the middle two points and take the average:

~~17, 25, 38,~~ 41, 42, ~~45, 46, 50~~

$(41 + 42) \div 2 = 41.5$

24. C)

Find Sam's income for each month:

January: $900

February: $1100

March: $500

April: $200

May: $400

Now find the average by adding those values and dividing by 5. Then round to the nearest 100: $\frac{900 + 1100 + 500 + 200 + 400}{5} = 620 \approx 600$

25. B)

Since there are 16 ounces in a pound, 8 ounces = 0.5 pounds. The conversion factor of kilograms to pounds is therefore multiplied by 8.5 pounds. The calculation is:

$8.5 \text{ lb.} \left(\frac{1 \text{kg}}{2.2 \text{ lb.}}\right) = \frac{8.5}{2.2} = 3.9 \text{ kg.}$

Notice that the 1 is on top in this conversion factor so that pounds cancel. The unit that the quantity is being converted to must always be in the numerator.

26. D)

To add or subtract numbers in scientific notation, the exponents of the base of 10 must be the same. The first number can be rewritten as $4.71 \times 10 \times 10^2 = 47.1 \times 10^2$. The values in front of 10^2 are subtracted, and the power of 10 stays the same, with a result of 44.12×10^2. The solution is then rewritten in proper scientific notation as 4.412×10^3.

27. B)

The answer choices are −6, 0, −11, and −30 for A), B), C), and D), respectively. Answer choice B), 0, is the only response that is not negative.

28. D)

The algebraic expression can be simplified using PEMDAS.

$10^2 - 7(3 - 4) - 25 \rightarrow$

$10^2 - 7(-1) - 25 \rightarrow$

$100 + 7 - 25 \rightarrow$

$107 - 25 \rightarrow$

82

29. B)

The algebraic expression can be simplified using PEMDAS.

$\frac{5^2(3) + 3(-2)^2}{4 + 3^2 - 2(5 - 8)} = \frac{5^2(3) + 3(-2)^2}{4 + 3^2 - 2(-3)} \rightarrow$

$\frac{25(3) + 3(4)}{4 + 9 - 2(-3)} = \frac{75 + 12}{13 + 6} = \frac{87}{19}$

30. C)

First convert everything to kilograms:

$800 \text{ g} \times \frac{1 \text{ kg}}{1,000 \text{ g}} = 0.8 \text{ kg}$

$300 \text{ g} \times \frac{1 \text{ kg}}{1,000 \text{ g}} = 0.3 \text{ kg}$

Next find the total weight:

$1.2 \text{ kg} + 0.8 \text{ kg} + 0.3 \text{ kg} = 2.3 \text{ kg}$

Now find the total cost by multiplying by $4/kg:

$2.3 \text{ kg} \times \frac{\$4}{1 \text{ kg}} = \$9.20$

31. B)

Each fraction is changed to an improper fraction: $\left(\frac{3}{2}\right)\left(\frac{8}{3}\right) \div \frac{5}{4}$.

Using PEMDAS and working left to right:

$\left(\frac{3}{2}\right)\left(\frac{8}{3}\right) \div \frac{5}{4} = \frac{24}{6} \div \frac{5}{4} = \frac{4}{1} \div \frac{5}{4}$.

To divide the fractions, the second fraction is flipped and then multiplied by the first fraction, giving $\left(\frac{4}{1}\right)\left(\frac{4}{5}\right) = \frac{16}{5}$.

This simplifies to $\frac{31}{5}$.

32. D)

First, simplify the exponents:

$2^{-1} = \frac{1}{2^1} = \frac{1}{2}$

$(-1)^3 = -1$

Now, order the quantities from most negative to most positive:

$-\frac{4}{3}, -1, \frac{2}{5}, \frac{1}{2}$

33. C)

The digit in the tenths place is 7 and is rounded up to 8 because the digit in the hundredths place is 8, which is greater than or equal to 5. So the number is rounded up to 2.8.

34. C)

A proportion is solved by cross-multiplying:

$5(4x - 5) = \frac{3}{2}(2x - 6)$

Then, the linear equation is solved for x:

$20x - 25 = 3x - 9; 17x = 16; x = \frac{16}{17}$.

35. D)

Start by adding 6 to both sides:

$8x - 6 + 6 = 3x + 24 + 6$

$8x = 3x + 30$

Next subtract $3x$ from both sides:

$8x - 3x = 3x + 30 - 3x$

$5x = 30$

Finally divide both sides by 5 to solve for x:

$5x \div 5 = 30 \div 5$

$x = 6$

36. D)

The solution can be written as a fraction by dividing the number of correct questions by the total number of questions: $\frac{42}{48} = 0.875$

Then, the result is multiplied by 100 for a grade of 87.5%.

37. D)

Substitute 5 for x:

$4(5) \div (5 - 1) = 20 \div 4 = 5$

38. C)

The slope of a horizontal line is zero because the change in y is zero.

39. C)

Alex and David split an appetizer that costs $8.50, so each will pay $4.25 in addition to the price of the entrée. Rachel orders an appetizer for $6.50, plus lemonade for $3, so she will pay $9.50 in addition to the price of the entrée.

$9.50 − $4.25 = $5.25

40. B)

Subtract the percentage of boys from 100% to find the percentage of girls:

100% − 46% = 54%

Find 21% of 54% of 450:

$0.21 \times 0.54 \times 450 \approx 51$

41. C)

First convert 15,140 drops to seconds using the ratio given:

$15{,}140 \text{ drops} \times \frac{4 \text{ sec.}}{1 \text{ drop}} = 60{,}560 \text{ sec.}$

Now convert seconds to hours:

$60{,}560 \text{ sec.} \times \frac{1 \text{ min.}}{60 \text{ sec.}} \times \frac{1 \text{ hr.}}{60 \text{ min.}} = 16.8\overline{2} \text{ hr.}$

Convert the remainder of hours back to minutes and seconds:

$0.8\overline{2} \text{ hr.} \times \frac{60 \text{ min.}}{1 \text{ hr.}} = 49.\overline{3} \text{ min.}$

$0.\overline{3} \text{ min.} \times \frac{60 \text{ sec.}}{1 \text{ min.}} = 20 \text{ sec.}$

16 hours, 49 minutes, 20 seconds

42. D)

First complete the operations in parentheses:
$(3 + 5)^2 + 24 \div 16 − 5 \div 2 = (8)^2 + 24 \div 16 − 5 \div 2$

Next solve the exponents: $(8)^2 + 24 \div 16 − 5 \div 2 = 64 + 24 \div 16 − 5 \div 2$

Then complete multiplication and division operations: $64 + 24 \div 16 − 5 \div 2 = 64 + 1.5 − 2.5$

Finally complete addition and subtraction operations: $64 + 1.5 − 2.5 = 63$

43. C)

First convert the length of the race to miles:
$10 \text{ km} \times \frac{1{,}000 \text{ m}}{1 \text{ km}} \times \frac{1 \text{ ft.}}{0.3048 \text{ m}} \times \frac{1 \text{ mi.}}{5280 \text{ ft.}} = 6.21 \text{ mi.}$

Next convert her training pace to minutes (in decimal form):

$15 \text{ sec.} \times \frac{1 \text{ min.}}{60 \text{ sec.}} = 0.25 \text{ min.}$

8 min., 15 sec. = 8 min. + 0.25 min. = 8.25 min.

Then multiply the length of the race by her pace per mile:

$6.21 \text{ mi.} \times \frac{8.25 \text{ min.}}{1 \text{ mi.}} = 51.23 \text{ min.}$

Finally convert the time back to min:sec form:

$0.23 \text{ min.} \times \frac{60 \text{ sec.}}{1 \text{ min.}} = 14 \text{ sec.}$

51:14

44. D)

Flip the divisor fraction and multiply:

$\frac{8}{15} \div \frac{1}{6} = \frac{8}{15} \times \frac{6}{1} = \frac{8 \times 6}{15 \times 1} = \frac{48}{15}$

Then reduce the fraction by dividing numerator and denominator by the greatest common factor:

$\frac{48}{15} = \frac{48 \div 3}{15 \div 3} = \frac{16}{5}$

Finally divide the whole numbers to find the mixed fraction:

$\frac{16}{5} = 3\frac{1}{5}$

45. A)

$5\frac{1}{3}$ tbsp. of lemon juice should be used.

Set up a ratio:

$\frac{2 \text{ tbsp.}}{\frac{1}{4} \text{ c.}} = \frac{x}{\frac{2}{3} \text{ c.}}$

Now cross-multiply:

$(2 \text{ tbsp.})\left(\frac{2}{3} \text{ c.}\right) = (x)\left(\frac{1}{4} \text{ c.}\right)$

$x = \frac{\left(2 \text{ tbsp.}\left(\frac{2}{3} \text{ c.}\right)\right)}{\frac{1}{4} \text{ c.}} = 5\frac{1}{3} \text{ tbsp.}$

46. C)

$x = \frac{\text{female 9th graders}}{\text{total 9th grades}}$ and $y = \frac{\text{total 9th graders}}{\text{total students}}$

You are looking for the proportion
$\frac{\text{female 9th graders}}{\text{total students}}$.

CONTINUE

See that multiplying x by y cancels out "total 9th graders" in the numerator and denominator and gives this proportion:

$$x \times y = \frac{\text{female 9th graders}}{\text{total 9th graders}} \times \frac{\text{total 9th graders}}{\text{total students}}$$

$$= \frac{\text{female 9th graders}}{\text{total students}}$$

47. A)

First calculate his original weekly work hours:

$$\frac{8 \text{ hr.}}{1 \text{ day}} \times \frac{5 \text{ days}}{1 \text{ wk.}} = \frac{40 \text{ hr.}}{\text{wk.}}$$

Next calculate his current weekly work hours:

$$\frac{8 \text{ hr}}{1 \text{day}} \times \frac{3 \text{ days}}{1 \text{ wk.}} + \frac{4 \text{ hr.}}{1 \text{ day}} \times \frac{2 \text{ days}}{1 \text{ wk.}} = \frac{32 \text{ hr.}}{\text{wk.}}$$

Now find the difference in hours and divide by his original hours to find the percentage change:

$$\frac{\frac{40 \text{ hr.}}{\text{wk.}} - \frac{32 \text{ hr.}}{\text{wk.}}}{\frac{40 \text{ hr.}}{\text{wk.}}} = \frac{x}{100}$$

$$\left(\frac{8 \text{ hr.}}{\text{wk.}}\right)(100) = \left(\frac{40 \text{ hr.}}{\text{wk.}}\right)(x)$$

$$x = \frac{\left(\frac{8 \text{ hr.}}{\text{wk.}}\right)(100)}{\left(\frac{40 \text{ hr.}}{\text{wk.}}\right)} = 20$$

Toledo's weekly work hours have decreased by 20%.

48. A)

Convert fractions to a common denominator and compare numerators:

$$\frac{2}{16} = \frac{6}{48}$$

$$\frac{1}{24} = \frac{2}{48}$$

$$\frac{3}{32} = \frac{4.5}{48}$$

$$\frac{3}{16} = \frac{9}{48}$$

$$\frac{2}{48} < \frac{4.5}{48} < \frac{5}{48} < \frac{6}{48} < \frac{9}{48}$$

49. A)

First subtract 4 from both sides:

$$3a + 4 - 4 = 2a - 4$$

$$3a = 2a - 4$$

Next subtract $2a$ from both sides (remember that the minus sign remains before the 4):

$$3a - 2a = 2a - 4 - 2a$$

$$a = -4$$

50. D)

A proportion is written using two ratios relating pages to minutes, with x representing the number of unknown minutes: $\frac{40}{45} = \frac{265}{x}$. The proportion is solved by cross-multiplying and dividing: $40x = 11{,}925$, $x = 298.125$. The solution is approximately 298 minutes.

51. D)

The money Jane earns is equal to $15 times the number of hours she babysits:

$15h$

The total money in Jane's bank account is equal to the money she started with plus the money she earns:

$275 + 15h$

Set this expression equal to $400:

$400 = 275 + 15h$

52. C)

This rectangular prism has 2 sides that are 12 inches by 18 inches, 2 sides that are 12 inches by 6 inches, and 2 sides that are 18 inches by 6 inches. Add the area of all the sides to find the total surface area:

$$SA = 2lw + 2lh + 2wh$$

$$SA = 2(12 \text{ in.})(18 \text{ in.}) + 2(12 \text{ in.})(6 \text{ in.}) + 2(18 \text{ in.})(6 \text{ in.})$$

$$SA = 432 \text{ in.}^2 + 144 \text{ in.}^2 + 216 \text{ in.}^2 = 792 \text{ in.}^2$$

53. C)

The answer choices are 24, −2, 30, and 0 for A, B, C, and D, respectively. Answer choice C, 30, is the greatest value for all of the responses.

54. B)

First find the radius of the pizza:

$$r = \frac{d}{2}$$

$$r = \frac{10 \text{ in.}}{2} = 5 \text{ in.}$$

Next use the formula for sector area:

$$A = \pi r^2 \frac{\theta}{360°}$$

$$A = \pi(5 \text{ in.})^2 \left(\frac{40°}{360°}\right) = 8.7 \text{ in.}^2$$

55. A)

The mean is equal to the sum of the results divided by the number of results:

$$\frac{1+3+5+x}{4} = 2.5$$

$1 + 3 + 5 + x = 10$

$x = 1$

56. C)

To find the mean, divide the sum of the data points by the number of data points:

Mean of seventh graders = $\frac{2+1+1+2+2}{5} = 1.6$

Mean of tenth graders = $\frac{0+1+1+0}{4} = 0.5$

Now find the difference:

$1.6 - 0.5 = 1.1$

57. D)

The conversion factor of meters to feet is multiplied by 55 meters. The calculation is

$55\,m\left(\frac{3.28\,ft.}{1\,m}\right) = 180.4$ feet

58. C)

The algebraic expression can be simplified using PEMDAS:

$-(3)^2 + (5-7)^2 - 3(4-8)$

$= -(3)^2 + (-2)^2 - 3(-4)$

$= -9 + 4 - 3(-4)$

$= -9 + 4 + 12$

$= 7$

59. B)

Divide the percentage who enrolled at a small public university by the total percentage who enrolled in a public university:

$$\frac{11\%}{11\% + 38\%} = 22\%$$

60. D)

The algebraic expression can be simplified using PEMDAS:

$(3^2 \div 1^3) - (4 - 8^2) + 2^4$

$= (9 \div 1) - (4 - 64) + 16$

$= 9 - (-60) + 16$

$= 85.$

61. B)

The first step is to subtract (resulting in −1.88); then add the result to 14.2 (making 12.32 the solution). Line up decimal points when adding or subtracting.

62. A)

First, find the radius:

$r = \frac{d}{2}$

$r = \frac{5\,in.}{2} = 2.5$ in.

Now use the formula for the volume of a cylinder:

$V = \pi r^2 h$

$V = \pi(2.5\,in.)^2(9\,in.) = 176.6\,in.^2$

63. B)

The least common denominator (LCD) for the three fractions is 120. To find the LCD, write each of the denominators in prime factorization form: $8 = 2^3$, $10 = 2 \times 5$, $3 = 3 \times 1$. The least common multiple of 8, 10, and 3 is the product of all the prime numbers in these factorizations to their highest power. So the LCD $= 2^3 \times 3 \times 5 = 120$.

To write each fraction in equivalent form with a denominator of 120, the first fraction is multiplied by $\frac{15}{15}$, the second fraction is multiplied by $\frac{12}{12}$, and the third fraction is multiplied by $\frac{40}{40}$. The problem is now:

$$\frac{105}{120} - \frac{12}{120} - \frac{80}{120} = \frac{93}{120} - \frac{80}{120} = \frac{13}{120}$$

64. D)

The fraction $\frac{10}{11}$ is changed to a decimal by long dividing 11 into 10 with the result of 0.909090... Therefore, the solution is $4.\overline{90}$ since the decimal repeats.

65. A)

The digit in the hundreds place is 3. It is rounded up to 4 because the digit in the tens place is 6, which is greater than or equal to 5. The number is thus rounded up to 74,400. The digit in the thousands place is 4, and remains 4 because the digit in the hundreds place (3) is less than 5. The number is therefore rounded to 74,000.

66. C)

The total amount of sales for the week is $2,700. The lowest amount of sales was on Tuesday and the largest was on Saturday. The ratio for Tuesday is $\frac{250}{2700} = \frac{5}{54}$ and the ratio for Saturday is $\frac{800}{2700} = \frac{8}{27}$.

67. B)

Start by combining like terms on each side:

$8y - 8 = 9y - 22$

Next, subtract $8y$ from both sides:

$8y - 8 - 8y = 9y - 22 - 8y$

$-8 = y - 22$

Finally, add 22 to both sides:

$-8 + 22 = y - 22 + 22$

$y = 14$

68. B)

Changing a percent to a decimal requires that the decimal point be moved two places to the left. Moving the decimal in 37.5 to the left two places results in 0.375.

69. D)

The first step is to find the amount of change by multiplying 37,500 by 0.055 (5.5% written as a decimal), which is $2,062.50. The amount of change, added to the original salary, is $39,562.50.

Alternatively, recognize the fact that the employee is now earning 105.5% of what he or she earned before. Calculate the new salary by multiplying $1.055 \times 37,500 = 39,562.50$.

70. D)

The values are easily compared if all are written in decimal form. The decimal values for D are -1.1, -0.8, -0.13, 0.7, and $.\overline{81}$. This is the only answer choice listed from least to greatest.

71. C)

The percent of change is the amount of change divided by the original amount, multiplied by 100. The amount of change is $7375 - 7250 = 125$. The percent change is $\frac{125}{7250} \times 100 = 1.7\%$.

72. B)

Since all the numerators are the same, the numbers can be ordered by comparing the denominators. The largest positive fractions have the smallest denominators (since dividing by larger numbers creates smaller fractions). For the negative fractions, the fraction closest to 0 (and therefore the largest) will be the one with the smallest absolute value (and largest denominator). Alternately, each of the fractions can be changed to decimals as $0.\overline{3}$, -0.25, 0.5, -0.2, $0.\overline{42857}$, $-0.\overline{16}$. The fractions written in order from greatest to least are

$\frac{1}{2}, \frac{1}{3}, \frac{1}{7}, -\frac{1}{6}, -\frac{1}{5}, -\frac{1}{4}.$

73. B)

First, take the additional 30% off the clearance price:

$\$65.00 \times \frac{70}{100} = \$45.50$

Next, find what percentage of $85.00 is $45.50:

$\frac{\$45.50}{\$85.00} = \frac{x}{100}$

$(\$45.50)(100) = (\$85.00)(x)$

$x = \frac{(\$45.50)(100)}{\$85.00} = 53.5$

Angie is paying 53.5% the original price, which means she received a $100\% - 53.5\% = 46.5\%$ discount.

74. D)

A rational number is one which can be written in the form of a simple fraction. If we observe closely, only option D) gives us a number which cannot be written in the form of a fraction.

75. C)

We are asked to round off this given number to the nearest hundredths place. Considering the numbers on the right of the decimal, our answer comes out to be 1230.93.

76. B)

We know that the absolute value of any negative number gives the positive of that same number (i.e. absolute value of -9 is $+9$).

77. C)

There are two ways to solve this question. First, you can add all the given numbers and find the exact answer. This method is time-consuming and is less efficient.

The second method to solve this question is by adding only the numbers on the left of the decimal and then comparing your answer with the answer choices that you are given. We add

45, 32, and 31 to get 45 + 32 + 31 = 108. Now, we can easily interpret that our answer must be very close to 108 when we add the decimal points as well for each given number. In the answer choices, only option C) gives us the number closest to 108. (Note that this method of approximation saves time but it is not very accurate if all the answer choices are very close to each other.)

78. B)

This is a very simple question. All you need to know is the PEMDAS rule. First of all, solve the problems inside the parentheses, and then we multiply the answers of each.

9 divided by 3 equals 3.

8 divided by 4 equals 2.

We multiply 3 and 2 to get our final answer: $3 \times 2 = 6$

79. B)

This is a simple division question. When we divide 7.95 by 1.5, we get 5.3 as answer. In order to re-confirm your answer, you can cross-check by multiplying 5.3 by 1.5, and it would be 7.95.

80. B)

There are twice as many red marbles as blue marbles, so (red) = 2(blue).

The number of blue marbles is 88% the number of green marbles, so (blue) = $0.88g$.

Substitute this expression for blue marbles in the one above:

(red) = $2(0.88g)$

(red) = $1.76g$

The total number of marbles is equal to red plus blue plus green:

(red) + (blue) + g

$1.76g + 0.88g + g$

$3.64g$

81. C)

Use the area to find the length of a side of the square:

$A = l \times w = l^2$

$5{,}625 \text{ ft}^2 = l^2$

$l = \sqrt{5{,}625 \text{ ft}^2} = 75 \text{ ft}$

Now multiply the side length by 4 to find the perimeter:

$P = 4l$

$P = 4(75 \text{ ft}) = 300 \text{ ft}$

82. C)

From the given information in the question, we know that 25% of the actual price of a desk is $45. If we write this in the form of an equation, it becomes:

$\left(\frac{25}{100}\right) \times x = \$45$ (25% of x equals $45)

$x = \frac{45}{0.25} \rightarrow \$180$

Therefore, the actual price of the desk equals $180.

83. B)

Multiply the ratios so that pants cancel out in the numerator and denominator:

$$\frac{4 \text{ shirts}}{1 \text{ pants}} \times \frac{5 \text{ pants}}{2 \text{ pairs shoes}} = \frac{20 \text{ shirts}}{2 \text{ pairs shoes}}$$

Divide by the greatest common factor to reduce the ratio:

$$\frac{20 \text{ shirts}}{2 \text{ pairs shoes}} \div 2 = \frac{10 \text{ shirts}}{1 \text{ pair shoes}}$$

84. C)

22 kg − 3.2 kg = 18.8 kg remaining for coffee

18.8 kg = 18,800 g

$$18{,}800 \text{ g} \times \frac{1 \text{ bag of coffee}}{800 \text{ g}} = 23.5 \text{ bags of coffee}$$

Round down to 23 bags.

85. C)

$0.28 = \frac{28}{100}$

The lowest common denominator is 4.

$\frac{28}{4} = 7$

$\frac{100}{4} = 25$

$= \frac{7}{25}$

READING

Directions: Read the question, passage, or figure carefully, and choose the best answer.

1. The social and political discourse of America continues to be permeated with idealism. An idealistic viewpoint asserts that the ideals of freedom, equality, justice, and human dignity are the truths that Americans must continue to aspire to. Idealists argue that truth is what should be, not necessarily what is. In general, they work to improve things and to make them as close to ideal as possible.

   Which of the following best captures the author's purpose?

   A) to advocate for freedom, equality, justice, and human rights

   B) to explain what an idealist believes in

   C) to explain what's wrong with social and political discourse in America

   D) to persuade readers to believe in certain truths

2. Examine the headings below. Based on the pattern, which of the following is a reasonable heading to insert in the blank spot?

   > **Chapter 3: Planning Your Vacation**
   > 1. Getting There
   >   A. Air Travel
   >   B. Traveling by Train
   >   C. _____
   >   D. Taking the Bus
   > 2. Accommodations
   > 3. Dining

   A) Choosing a Destination

   B) Navigating the Airport

   C) Finding a Hotel

   D) Road Trips

The next four questions are based on this passage.

The best friend a man has in the world may turn against him and become his enemy. His son or daughter that he has reared with loving care may prove ungrateful. Those who are nearest and dearest to us, those whom we trust with our happiness and our good name may become traitors to their faith. The money that a man has, he may lose. It flies away from him, perhaps when he needs it most. A man's reputation may be sacrificed in a moment of ill-considered action.

The one absolutely unselfish friend that man can have in this selfish world, the one that never deserts him, the one that never proves ungrateful or treacherous is his dog. A man's dog stands by him in prosperity and in poverty, in health and in sickness. He will sleep on the cold ground, where the wintry winds blow and the snow drives fiercely, if only he may be near his master's side. He will kiss the hand that has no food to offer. He will lick the wounds and sores that come in encounters with the roughness of the world. He guards the sleep of his pauper master as if he were a prince. When all other friends desert, he remains.

George Graham Vest - c. 1855
http://www.historyplace.com/speeches/vest.htm

3. Which of the following best describes the structure of the text?

   A) chronology

   B) cause and effect

   C) problem and solution

   D) contrast

4. Which of the following could be considered the topic of this passage?

   A) loyal friends

   B) misfortune

   C) human treachery

   D) feeling safe

5. Which of the following is a logical conclusion of the passage?

   A) Those closest to you will always betray you.

   B) Friendships with other people are pointless.

   C) Someone who wants a loyal friend should get a dog.

   D) Only a dog can help a person through the rough times in his or her life.

6. Which of the following is the purpose of this passage?

   A) to inform

   B) to entertain

   C) to describe

   D) to persuade

The next two questions are based on this passage.

> ### How to Plant Potatoes
> **Before Planting**
>
> Plant potatoes no later than 2 weeks after the last spring freeze.
>
> Cut potatoes into pieces 1 to 2 days before planting.
>
> Loosen soil using a tiller or hand trowel.
>
> Mix fertilizer or compost into loosened soil.
>
> **Planting**
>
> Dig a 4-inch-deep trench and place potatoes 1 foot apart.
>
> Cover potatoes loosely with soil.
>
> **After Planting**
>
> Water immediately after planting, and then regularly afterward to keep soil moist.
>
> After 6 weeks, mound soil around the base of the plant to ensure roots stay covered.

7. Which of the following is the first step to take after planting potatoes?

   A) Mound soil around the base of the plant.

   B) Water immediately.

   C) Mix fertilizer or compost into loosened soil.

   D) Place potatoes 1 foot apart.

8. Which of the following should be done after the soil has been loosened with a tiller or trowel?

   A) Mix fertilizer or compost into loosened soil.

   B) Dig a 4-inch-deep trench.

   C) Cut potatoes into pieces.

   D) Mound soil around the base of the plant.

The next two questions are based on this email.

Alan —

   I just wanted to drop you a quick note to let you know I'll be out of the office for the next two weeks. Elizabeth and I are finally taking that trip to France we've been talking about for years. It's a bit of a last-minute decision, but since we had the vacation time available, we figured it was now or never.

   Anyway, my team's been briefed on the upcoming meeting, so they should be able to handle the presentation without any hiccups. If you have any questions or concerns, you can direct them to Joanie, who'll be handling my responsibilities while I'm out.

   Let me know if you want any special treats. I don't know if you can take chocolate and cheese on the plane, but I'm going to try!

   Best regards,

   Michael

9. Which of the following most likely describes the relationship between the author and Alan?

   A) familial

   B) formal

   C) friendly

   D) strained

10. Which of the following best captures the author's purpose?

   A) to ask Alan if he wants any special treats from France

   B) to brag to Alan about his upcoming vacation

   C) to inform Alan that he will be out of the office

   D) to help Alan prepare for the upcoming meeting

→

CONTINUE

The next two questions are based on this map.

11. Which of the following is located due north of the Fire Circle?

A) Old Oak Tree

B) Scout Camp

C) Fishing Pond

D) Backcountry Camping

12. If a camper followed the trail from the Fishing Pond to the Scout Camp and passed by the Fire Circle, which of the following would she also have to pass by?

A) Old Oak Tree

B) Ranger Station

C) Backcountry Camping

D) Pier

The next three questions are based on this passage.

Carl's Car Depot is hosting its one-day-only summer sale event! All sedans, trucks, SUVs, and more are marked to move quickly. We're offering no money down and low (like, really low) monthly payments. You won't find prices like these anywhere else in the city (or the state, or anywhere else you look). No matter what you're looking for, we've the new and used cars you need. We only drop our prices this low once a year, so don't miss out on this great deal!

13. Which of the following best describes the author's purpose?

A) The author wants to tell customers what kinds of cars are available at Carl's Car Depot.

B) The author wants to encourage other car dealerships to lower their prices.

C) The author wants to provide new and used cars at affordable prices.

D) The author wants to attract customers to Carl's Car Depot.

14. Based on the context, which of the following is the meaning of the word *move* in the passage?

A) drive

B) sell

C) advance forward

D) change location

15. Which of the following is NOT mentioned by the author as a reason to visit Carl's Car Depot?

A) They are offering lifetime warranties on new cars.

B) The sale will only last one day.

C) They have the lowest prices in town.

D) They are offering no money down and low monthly payments.

16. Although Ben *said* he supported for his coworkers, his actions suggested he did not condone their behavior.

Italics are used for which of the following reasons?

A) to show a word is intentionally misspelled

B) to indicate a word in a foreign language

C) to emphasize a contrast

D) to reference a footnote

The next five questions are based on this passage.

It had been a long morning for Julia. She'd been woken up early by the sound of lawn mowers outside her window, and despite her best efforts, had been unable to get back to sleep. So, she'd reluctantly got out of bed, showered, and prepared her morning cup of coffee. At least, she tried to anyway. In the kitchen she'd discovered she was out of regular coffee and had to settle for a decaffeinated cup instead.

Once on the road, her caffeine-free mug of coffee didn't help make traffic less annoying. In fact, it seemed to Julia like the other drivers were sluggish and surly as well—it took her an extra fifteen minutes to get to work. And when she arrived, all the parking spots were full.

By the time she'd finally found a spot in the overflow lot, she was thirty minutes late for work. She'd hoped her boss would be too busy to notice, but he'd already put a pile of paperwork on her desk with a note that simply said "Rewrite." She wondered if she should point out to her boss that she hadn't been the one to write the reports in the first place, but decided against it.

When the fire alarm went off an hour later, Julia decided she'd had enough. She grabbed her purse and headed outside with her coworkers. While everyone else stood around waiting for the alarm to quiet, Julia determinedly walked to her car, fired up the engine, and set a course for home.

17. Which of the following lists Julia's actions in the correct sequence?

A) Julia woke up early and found she didn't have any regular coffee. When she got to work, her boss had a lot for her to do. When the fire alarm went off, she decided to go home.

B) Julia got to work and decided she was too tired to do the work her boss asked for, so she went home to get a cup of coffee.

C) Julia woke up when the fire alarm went off and couldn't get back to sleep. She then got stuck in traffic and arrived at work thirty minutes late.

D) Julia was woken up early by a lawnmower and then got stuck in traffic on the way to her office. Once there, she found that the office was out of coffee and she had a lot of work to do. When the fire alarm went off, she decided to go home.

18. Which of the following is the most likely reason Julia did not return to work after the alarm?

A) She was embarrassed that should could not finish the work her boss asked for.

B) She was tired and wanted to go home.

C) She got stuck in traffic and could not get back to her office.

D) Her boss gave her the afternoon off.

19. Which of the following statements based on the passage should be considered an opinion?

A) Julia's boss asked her to do work to help one of her coworkers.

B) Julia was late to work because of traffic.

C) It was irresponsible for Julia to leave work early.

D) Julia was tired because she'd been woken up early.

20. The passage states that Julia *set a course for home*. Which of the following is the most accurate interpretation of this sentence?

    A) Julia is looking up directions to her house.

    B) Julia is planning to drive home.

    C) Julia wants to go home but will go back to work.

    D) Julia is worried the fire at her office will spread to her home.

21. Which of the following conclusions is best supported by the passage?

    A) Julia will find a job closer to her home.

    B) Julia will be fired.

    C) Julia will feel guilty and return to work.

    D) Julia will drive home and go to sleep.

22. Alexander Hamilton and James Madison called for the Constitutional Convention to write a constitution as the foundation of a stronger federal government. Madison and other Federalists like John Adams believed in separation of powers, republicanism, and a strong federal government. Despite the separation of powers that would be provided for in the US Constitution, anti-Federalists like Thomas Jefferson called for even more limitations on the power of the federal government.

    In the context of the passage above, which of the following would most likely NOT support a strong federal government?

    A) Alexander Hamilton

    B) James Madison

    C) John Adams

    D) Thomas Jefferson

23. Based on the pattern in the headings, which of the following is a reasonable heading to insert in the blank spot?

Chapter 2: Amphibians of Texas
1.   Frogs
A) Tree Frogs
B) _____
C) True Frogs
2.   Toads
A) True Toads
B) Narrowmouth Toads
C) Burrowing Toads
3.   Salamanders

    A) Gray Tree Frog

    B) Tropical Frogs

    C) Newts

    D) Spadefoot Toads

24. Which of the following is an example of a secondary source that would be used in a documentary about World War I?

    A) an essay by a historian about the lasting effects of the war

    B) photographs of military equipment used in the war

    C) a recorded interview with a veteran who fought for the US Army

    D) letters written by soldiers to their families

25. Victoria won easily and had plenty of time to rest before her next scheduled match.

    Based on the context, which of the following is the meaning of the word *match* in the sentence?

    A) a competitive event

    B) a suitable pair

    C) a slender piece of wood used to start a fire

    D) a prospective marriage partner

The next two questions are based on this table.

Table 1.1. Book Sales by Distributor

DISTRIBUTOR	COST STRUCTURE
Wholesale Books	$100 for the first 25 books; $80 for every 25 additional books
The Book Barn	$98 for every 25 books
Books and More	$3.99 per book
Quarter Price Books	$3.99 per book for the first 25 books; $2.99 for each additional book

26. A school wants to buy seventy-five textbooks. Based on the pricing chart, which of the following distributors would offer the cheapest price for the books?

A) Wholesale Books

B) The Book Barn

C) Books and More

D) Quarter Price Books

27. A teacher wants to buy an additional twenty-five books for her classroom. If she orders her books separately, which distributor would offer the cheapest price?

A) Wholesale Books

B) The Book Barn

C) Books and More

D) Quarter Price Books

The next two questions are based on this passage.

The study showed that private tutoring is providing a significant advantage to those students who are able to afford it. Researchers looked at the grades of students who had received free tutoring through the school versus those whose parents had paid for private tutors. The study included 2500 students in three high schools across four grade levels. The study found that private tutoring corresponded with a rise in grade point average (GPA) of 0.5 compared to students who used the school's free tutor service and 0.7 compared to students who used no tutoring. After reviewing the study, the board is recommending that the school restructure its free tutor service to provide a more equitable education for all students.

28. Which of the following would weaken the author's argument?

A) the fact that the cited study was funded by a company that provides discounted tutoring through schools

B) a study showing differences in standardized test scores between students at schools in different neighborhoods

C) a statement signed by local teachers stating that they do not provide preferential treatment in the classroom or when grading

D) a study showing that GPA does not strongly correlate with success in college

29. Which of the following types of arguments is used in the passage?

A) emotional argument

B) appeal to authority

C) specific evidence

D) rhetorical questioning

CONTINUE

30. Start with the shapes shown below. Follow the directions.

A B C D E F

1. Remove block C.
2. Remove block E.
3. Place block A immediately after block D.
4. Add block C after block A.

Which of the following shows the order in which the shapes now appear?

A) B D A F

B) B D A E F

C) B D A C F

D) B D F A C

The next two questions are based on this passage.

After looking at five houses, Robert and I have decided to buy the one on Forest Road. The first two homes we visited didn't have the space we need—the first had only one bathroom, and the second did not have a guest bedroom. The third house, on Pine Street, had enough space inside but didn't have a big enough yard for our three dogs. The fourth house we looked at, on Rice Avenue, was stunning but well above our price range. The last home, on Forest Road, wasn't in the neighborhood we wanted to live in. However, it had the right amount of space for the right price.

31. Which of the following lists the author's actions in the correct sequence?

A) The author looked at the house on Forest Road, then at a house with a yard that was too small, then at two houses that were too small, and then finally at a house that was too expensive.

B) The author looked at the house on Forest Road, then at two houses that were too small, then at a house with a yard that was too small, and then finally at a house that was too expensive.

C) The author looked at two homes with yards that were too small, then a house with only one bathroom, then a house that was too expensive, and then finally the house on Forest Road.

D) The author looked at two homes that were too small, then a house with a yard that was too small, then a house that was too expensive, and then finally at the house on Forest Road.

32. What is the author's conclusion about the house on Pine Street?

A) The house did not have enough bedrooms.

B) The house did not have a big enough yard.

C) The house was not in the right neighborhood.

D) The house was too expensive.

33. A student wants to find unbiased information on an upcoming state senate election for a class project. Which of the following sources should the student use?

A) a website run by a candidate's campaign advisor

B) an endorsement of a candidate from a local newspaper

C) a blog run by a local radio personality

D) a book on the history of elections

The next two questions are based on this passage.

Mr. Tim Morgan —

This letter is to inform Mr. Morgan that his application for the position of Lead Technician has been received by our Human Resources team. We have been pleased to receive a higher-than-expected number of applications for this position, and we are glad that Mr. Morgan is among the many who find our company an attractive place to build a career. Due to the influx of applications, our Human Resources team will be taking

> longer than previously stated to review candidates and schedule interviews. Please look for further communication from our Human Resources team in the next two to three weeks.
>
> Regards,
>
> Allison Wakefield
> Head of Human Resources

34. Which of the following best describes the purpose of the passage?

A) to let Mr. Morgan know that he will likely not receive an offer for the job of Lead Technician due to the high number of applicants

B) to express to Mr. Morgan how pleased the Human Resources team was to receive his application

C) to offer Mr. Morgan the position of Lead Technician

D) to inform Mr. Morgan that the review of candidates will take longer than expected

35. Which of the following conclusions is well supported by the passage?

A) The Human Resources team had previously informed Mr. Morgan that he would receive feedback on his application in less than two weeks.

B) Mr. Morgan is well qualified for the position of Lead Technician and will be offered an interview.

C) The Human Resources team will have trouble finding a qualified candidate for the position of Lead Technician.

D) Mr. Morgan will respond to this communication by removing himself from consideration for the positon of Lead Technician.

The next three questions are based on this passage.

The greatest changes in sensory, motor, and perceptual development happen in the first two years of life. When babies are first born, most of their senses operate in a similar way to those of adults. For example, babies are able to hear before they are born; studies show that babies turn toward the sound of their mothers' voices just minutes after being born, indicating they recognize the mother's voice from their time in the womb.

The exception to this rule is vision. A baby's vision changes significantly in its first year of life; initially it has a range of vision of only 8 – 12 inches and no depth perception. As a result, infants rely primarily on hearing; vision does not become the dominant sense until around the age of 12 months. Babies also prefer faces to other objects. This preference, along with their limited vision range, means that their sight is initially focused on their caregiver.

36. Which of the following is a concise summary of the passage?

A) Babies have no depth perception until 12 months, which is why they focus only on their caregivers' faces.

B) Babies can recognize their mothers' voices when born, so they initially rely primarily on their sense of hearing.

C) Babies have senses similar to those of adults except for their sense of sight, which doesn't fully develop until 12 months.

D) Babies' senses go through many changes in the first year of their lives.

37. Which of the following senses do babies primarily rely on?

A) vision

B) hearing

C) touch

D) smell

38. Which of the following best describes the mode of the passage?

A) expository

B) narrative

C) persuasive

D) descriptive

39. According to the guide, in which of the following seasons would ginger be harvested?

> **Spring**: artichokes, broccoli, chives, collard greens, peas, spinach, watercress
>
> **Summer**: beets, bell peppers, corn, eggplant, green beans, okra, tomatoes, zucchini
>
> **Fall**: acorn squash, brussels sprouts, cauliflower, endive, ginger, sweet potatoes
>
> **Winter**: Belgian endive, buttercup squash, kale, leeks, turnips, winter squash

A) spring

B) summer

C) fall

D) winter

40. Based on the pattern in the headings, which of the following is a reasonable heading to insert in the blank spot?

> 3. Balanced Nutrition
>   A. Sources of iron
>   1) Animal-based sources
>   a. Beef
>   b. Pork
>   c. _____
>   2) Plant-based sources
>   a. Leafy greens
>   b. Nuts and seeds
>   B. Sources of calcium

A) Dairy

B) Lamb

C) Legumes

D) Vitamins

The next two questions are based on this passage.

In Greek mythology, two gods, Epimetheus and Prometheus, were given the work of creating living things. Epimetheus gave good powers to the different animals. To the lion he gave strength; to the bird, swiftness; to the fox, sagacity; and so on. Eventually, all of the good gifts had been bestowed, and there was nothing left for humans. As a result, Prometheus returned to heaven and brought down fire, which he gave to humans. With fire, human beings could protect themselves by making weapons. Over time, humans developed civilization.

41. Which of the following provides the best summary of the passage?

A) Epimetheus was asked to assign all the good traits to the animals, which upset Prometheus. In retaliation, Prometheus brought fire to humans, which allowed them to reign over the other animals.

B) Epimetheus and Prometheus were both asked to create living things and assign traits to living creatures. Epimetheus gave all of the positive traits to the other animals and left nothing for humans, so Prometheus brought humans fire. This fire allowed human beings to thrive.

C) Epimetheus and Prometheus were given the job of assigning traits to the animals. They decided to give strength to lions, swiftness to birds, sagacity to the fox, and fire to humans. This fire has helped humans grow to be superior to other animals.

D) Prometheus decided that humans needed fire to protect themselves from the other animals. He brought fire down from Heaven and taught humans how to make weapons, which allowed humans to hunt animals.

42. Which of the following is the meaning of the word *bestowed* as it is used in the passage?

A) purchased

B) forgotten

C) accepted

D) given

The next two questions are based on this excerpt.

Table of Contents

1. Renaissance Art ....15 – 104

   A)   Italian Painters ....18 – 57

   B)   German Painters ....59 – 72

   C)   French Painters ....73 – 104

2. Renaissance Architecture .... 105 – 203

   A)   Renaissance: 1400 – 1500 ....107 – 152

   B)   High Renaissance: 1500 – 1525 ....153 – 177

   C)   Mannerism: 1520 – 1600 ....179 – 203

43. A student wants to find information on the Italian painter Sandro Botticelli. On which of the following pages will the student most likely find this information?

A) 55

B) 71

C) 95

D) 114

44. A student wants to find information on a church built in 1518. On which of the following pages should the student begin to look for this information?

A) 59

B) 105

C) 153

D) 179

The next two questions are based on this passage.

As you can see from the graph, my babysitting business has been really successful. The year started with a busy couple of months—several snows combined with a large number of requests for Valentine's Day services boosted our sales quite a bit. The spring months have admittedly been a bit slow, but we're hoping for a big summer once school gets out. Several clients have already put in requests for our services!

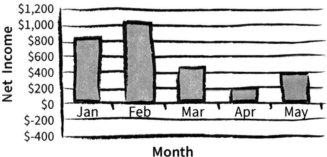

Sam's Net Income by Month

45. Based on the information in the graph, how much more did Sam's Babysitting Service bring in during February than during April?

A) $200

B) $900

C) $1100

D) $1300

46. Which of the following best describes the tone of the passage?

A) professional

B) casual

C) concerned

D) neutral

The next two questions are based on this passage.

The odds of success for any new restaurant are slim. Competition in the city is fierce, and the low margin of return means that aspiring restaurateurs must be exact and ruthless with their budget and pricing. The fact that The Hot Dog has lasted as long as it has is a testament to its owners' skills.

47. Which of the following conclusions is well supported by the passage?

    A) The Hot Dog offers the best casual dining in town.

    B) The Hot Dog has a well-managed budget and prices items on its menu appropriately.

    C) The popularity of The Hot Dog will likely fall as new restaurants open in the city.

    D) The Hot Dog has a larger margin of return than other restaurants in the city.

48. Which of the following is the meaning of *testament* as used in the sentence?

    A) story

    B) surprise

    C) artifact

    D) evidence

49. Which of the following sentences indicates the end of a sequence?

    A) Our ultimate objective was to find a quality coat at an affordable price.

    B) We chose this particular restaurant because of its outdoor seating.

    C) Finally, we were able to settle in to enjoy the movie.

    D) Initially, it seemed unlikely that we'd be able to keep the puppy.

50. When connecting line A to port B, make sure that port C is **completely** closed. If port C is left open, fluid will leak as soon as line A is connected. Once line A and port B are **fully** connected, port C can be opened as needed.

    The bold text in the directions above indicate which of the following?

    A) brand names

    B) emphasis

    C) commands

    D) proper nouns

51. A student wants to find information on the Battle of the Scheldt. According to the index for a history textbook, where should the student look?

Battle of San Marino	112 – 3, 201
Battle of Sedan	113, 202
Battle of Sidi Barrani	115 – 6
Battle of Someri	203 – 205
Battle of Stalingrad	306 – 310
Battle of Studzianki	307 – 308
Battle of the Scheldt	110 – 2, 207

    A) 110

    B) 115

    C) 203

    D) 307

The next three questions are based on this passage.

In its most basic form, geography is the study of space; more specifically, it studies the physical space of the earth and the ways in which it interacts with, shapes, and is shaped by its habitants. Geographers look at the world from a spatial perspective. This means that at the center of all geographic study is the question, where? For geographers, the where of any interaction, event, or development is a crucial element to understanding it.

This question of where can be asked in a variety of fields of study, so there are many sub-disciplines of geography. These can be organized into four main categories: 1) regional studies, which examine the characteristics of a particular place, 2) topical studies, which look at a single physical or human feature that impacts the whole world, 3) physical studies, which focus on the physical features of Earth, and 4) human studies, which examine the relationship between human activity and the environment.

52. A researcher studying the relationship between farming and river systems would be engaged in which of the following geographical sub-disciplines?

A) regional studies

B) topical studies

C) physical studies

D) human studies

53. Which of the following best describes the mode of the passage?

A) expository

B) narrative

C) persuasive

D) descriptive

54. Which of the following is a concise summary of the passage?

A) The most important questions in geography are where an event or development took place.

B) Geography, which is the study of the physical space on earth, can be broken down into four sub-disciplines.

C) Regional studies is the study of a single region or area.

D) Geography can be broken down into four sub-disciplines: regional studies, topical studies, physical studies, and human studies.

The next three questions are based on this passage.

It's that time again—the annual Friendswood Village Summer Fair is here! Last year we had a record number of visitors, and we're expecting an even bigger turnout this year. The fair will be bringing back all our traditional food and games, including the famous raffle. This year, we'll have a carousel, petting zoo, and climbing wall (for teenagers and adults only, please). We're also excited to welcome Petey's BBQ and Happy Tummy's Frozen Treats, who are both new to the fair this year. Tickets are available online and at local retailers.

55. Which of the following will NOT be a new presence at the Fair this year?

A) the raffle

B) the petting zoo

C) the carousel

D) Petey's BBQ

56. Based on the context, which of the following is the meaning of the word *record* in the passage?

A) a piece of evidence

B) a disk with a groove that reproduces sound

C) the best or most remarkable

D) to set down in writing

57. Which of the following best describes the mode of the passage?

A) expository

B) narrative

C) persuasive

D) descriptive

⟶ CONTINUE

58. Based on the pattern in the headings, which of the following is a reasonable heading to insert in the blank spot?

> **Chapter 3. Emotions and the Central Nervous System**
>
> 3A. Involuntary Physical Symptoms of Emotion
>
>   a) Flushing
>
>   b) _____
>
>   c) Vocal Changes
>
> 3B. Voluntary Physical Response to Emotion
>
> 3C. Conscious Control of Emotions

A) Facial Expressions

B) Happiness

C) Emotions and Central Nervous System Disorders

D) The Cerebral Cortex

59. Based on the pattern in the headings, which of the following is a reasonable heading to insert in the blank spot?

> **I. Types of Teas**
>
> A.   Black Tea
>
>   a) Assam
>
>   b) Darjeeling
>
>   c) Ceylong
>
> B.   _____
>
> C.   White Tea

A) Green Tea

B) Iced Tea

C) Cold-Brew Tea

D) Chai Tea

The next two questions are based on the table of contents below.

Table of Contents

3. The Cold War ....153 – 306

    A)   The End of World War II ....153 – 175

    B)   Escalation ....176 – 258

    C)   Détente and the Final Years ....259 – 306

4. The Cold War in Popular Culture ....307 – 394

    A)   Contemporary Depictions of the Cold War (1945 – 1991) ....307 – 363

    B)   Modern Depictions of the Cold War (1992 – 2015) ....364 – 394

60. A student wants to find information on how the Potsdam Treaty, signed at the end of World War II, affected the Cold War. On which of the following pages will the student most likely find this information?

A) 155

B) 256

C) 308

D) 383

61. A researcher wants to find information on a movie made in 1967 about the Cold War. On which of the following pages should the researcher look for this information?

A) 168

B) 300

C) 311

D) 370

The next three questions are based on this passage.

Alexis de Tocqueville, a young Frenchman from an aristocratic family, visited the United States in the early 1800s. He observed: "Amongst the novel objects that attracted my attention during my stay in the United States, nothing struck me more forcibly than the general equality of conditions. [...] The more I advanced in the study of American society, the more I perceived that the equality of conditions is the fundamental fact from which all others seem to be derived, and the central point at which all my observations constantly terminated."

Excerpt from Alexis de Tocqueville's *Democracy in America*, 1835

62. Which of the following best states the main idea of the passage?

   A) Alexis de Tocqueville has contributed substantially to the study of the nineteenth-century United States.

   B) Equality was the most important ideal in the nineteenth-century United States.

   C) In nineteenth-century American society, all people had rights.

   D) American society during the nineteenth century was more equal than French society.

63. Based on the context, which of the following is the meaning of the word *novel* in the passage?

   A) new

   B) written

   C) uncertain

   D) confusing

64. Which of the following is an example of a primary source that would be used in a research paper on the history of mining in West Virginia?

   A) a book written by a modern historian on the growth of American unions

   B) letters written by a miner to his family in New York

   C) a recent documentary on historical mining equipment

   D) a historical novel set in a mining camp in West Virginia

65. The author would most likely agree with which of the following statements about the United States in the nineteenth century?

   A) Right from the beginning at least three social classes emerged, with most people falling in the middle.

   B) American people were by nature competitive and individualistic.

   C) Since the birth of the United States, its citizens have been eager to achieve and prosper.

   D) In the early decades when America had just become an independent country with a new government, people lived in equality.

66. Spanish *conquistadors* explored what is today the Southwest United States, claiming land for Spain despite the presence of southwestern tribes.

   Italics are used in the passage above for which of the following reasons?

   A) to show that a word is intentionally misspelled

   B) to indicate a word in a foreign language

   C) to emphasize a contrast

   D) to reference a footnote

67. The strange light in the room made it hard to determine the colors used in the painting.

   Based on the context of the passage above, which of the following is the meaning of the word *light* in the sentence?

   A) a sense of mental illumination or enlightenment

   B) the electromagnetic waves that make human vision possible

   C) a device used to indicate right of way for traffic

   D) to start a fire

The next two questions are based on this map.

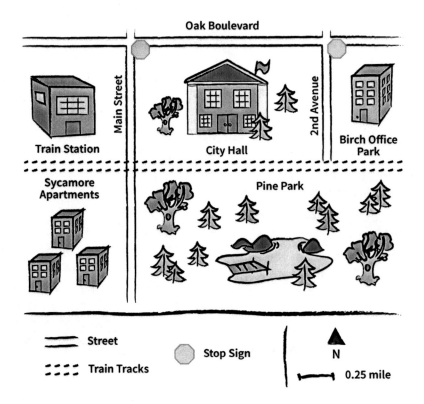

68. A family leaves the train station and heads south on Main Street. At which of the following locations will the train arrive?

    A) City Hall

    B) Oak Boulevard

    C) Sycamore Apartments

    D) Birch Office Park

69. According to the map, which of the following is the distance from City Hall to the Birch Office Park?

    A) 0.1 miles

    B) 1 mile

    C) 10 miles

    D) 100 miles

The next five questions are based on this passage.

The most important part of brewing coffee is getting the right water. Choose a water that you think has a nice, neutral flavor. Anything with too many minerals or contaminants will change the flavor of the coffee, and water with too few minerals won't do a good job of extracting the flavor from the coffee beans. Water should be heated to between 195 and 205 degrees Fahrenheit. Boiling water (212 degrees Fahrenheit) will burn the beans and give your coffee a scorched flavor.

While the water is heating, grind your beans. Remember, the fresher the grind, the fresher the flavor of the coffee. The number of beans is entirely dependent on your personal taste. Obviously, more beans will result in a more robust flavor, while fewer beans will give your coffee a more subtle taste. The texture of the grind should be not too fine (which can lead to bitter coffee) or too large (which can lead to weak coffee).

Once the beans are ground and the water has reached the perfect temperature, you're ready to brew. A French press (which we recommend), allows you to control brewing time and provide a thorough brew. Pour the grounds into the press, then pour the hot water over the grounds and let it steep. The brew shouldn't require more than 5 minutes, although those of you who like your coffee a bit harsher can leave it longer. Finally, use the plunger to remove the grounds and pour.

70. According to the passage, which of the following lists the steps for brewing coffee in the correct sequence?

  A) Choose a water that doesn't have too many or two few minerals. Then, heat water to boiling and pour over coffee grounds.

  B) Ground the beans to the appropriate texture and pour into the French press. Then, heat water to boiling and pour over the ground beans. Finally, use the plunger to remove the grounds and pour.

  C) Ground beans to the appropriate texture, and then heat water to 195 degrees Fahrenheit. Next, pour water over the grounds and steep for no more than five minutes. Finally, remove the grounds using the plunger.

  D) Choose the right type of water and heat it to the correct temperature. Next, ground the beans and put them in the French press. Then, pour the hot water over the grounds and let the coffee steep.

71. Which of the following statements based on the passage should be considered an opinion?

  A) While the water is heating, grind your beans.

  B) A French press (which we recommend), allows you to control brewing time and provide a thorough brew.

  C) Anything with too many minerals or contaminants will change the flavor of the coffee, and water with too few minerals won't do a good job of extracting the flavor from the coffee beans.

  D) Finally, use the plunger to remove the grounds and pour.

72. Which of the following best describes the structure of the text?

  A) chronological

  B) cause and effect

  C) problem and solution

  D) contrast

73. Which of the following conclusions is best supported by the passage?

  A) Coffee should never be brewed for longer than 5 minutes.

  B) It's better to use too many coffee beans when making coffee than too few.

  C) Brewing quality coffee at home is too complicated for most people to do well.

  D) The best way to brew coffee is often determined by personal preferences.

74. Which of the following would be an appropriate title for this passage?

  A) How to Brew the Perfect Cup of Coffee

  B) Why Drinking Coffee Is the Best Way to Start the Day

  C) How to Use a French Press to Make Coffee

  D) The Importance of Grinding Coffee Beans

The next two questions are based on this passage.

For an adult person to be unable to swim points to something like criminal negligence; every man, woman and child should learn. A person who cannot swim may not only become a danger to himself, but to someone, and perhaps to several, of his fellow beings. Children as early as the age of four may acquire the art; none are too young, none too old.

Frank Eugen Dalton, *Swimming Scientifically Taught*, 1912

75. Which of the following best captures the author's purpose?

- **A)** to encourage the reader to learn to swim
- **B)** to explain how people who cannot swim are a danger to others
- **C)** to inform the reader that it's never too late to learn to swim
- **D)** to argue that people who cannot swim should be punished

76. Which of the following is the purpose of this passage?

- **A)** to inform
- **B)** to entertain
- **C)** to describe
- **D)** to persuade

The next three questions are based on this passage.

New Policy for Replacement Student Identification Cards

Due to recent issues with the abuse of student identification (ID) cards, Campus Security has issued a new policy for acquiring replacement student identification cards.

The following conditions must be met for students to receive a replacement student ID card:

- ◆ Student is currently enrolled in at least one class; the class may be either online or on campus.
- ◆ Student must have been issued a student ID card within the last five years.
- ◆ Student must apply for a replacement ID card in person at the Student Admissions Office. Online applications will no longer be accepted.
- ◆ Students will be required to pay a $25 fee for each replacement ID card. Fee may not be charged to the student's account.

Students who do not meet these conditions will be required to apply for a new ID card at the Campus Security Office.

77. Based on the context, which of the following is the meaning of the word *abuse* in the passage?

- **A)** failure
- **B)** punishment
- **C)** misuse
- **D)** disappearance

78. Which of the following would not be eligible to receive a replacement student ID card from the Student Admissions Office?

- **A)** a student enrolled in one online class
- **B)** a student who lives abroad and must apply for her replacement student ID online
- **C)** a currently enrolled student who has lost his student ID card
- **D)** a student who has reenrolled after a three year absence from the school

79. Which of the following best describes the purpose of this passage?

- **A)** to ensure that students pay the appropriate fee when applying for a replacement ID card
- **B)** to inform students of the new policy regarding replacement ID cards
- **C)** to inform online students that they will no longer be eligible to receive replacement ID cards
- **D)** to punish students who have used student ID cards incorrectly in the past

The next three questions are based on this passage.

Alfie closed his eyes and took several deep breaths. He was trying to ignore the sounds of the crowd, but even he had to admit that it was hard not to notice the tension in the stadium. He could feel 50,000 sets of eyes burning through his skin—this crowd expected perfection from him. He took another breath and opened his eyes, setting his sights on the soccer ball resting peacefully in the grass. One shot, just one last shot, between his team and the championship. He didn't look up at the goalie, who was jumping nervously on the goal line just a few yards away. Afterward, he would swear he didn't remember anything between the referee's whistle and the thunderous roar of the crowd.

80. Which of the following conclusions is best supported by the passage?

    A) Alfie passed out on the field and was unable to take the shot.

    B) The goalie blocked Alfie's shot.

    C) Alfie scored the goal and won his team the championship.

    D) The referee declared the game a tie.

81. Which of the following best describes the meaning of the phrase "he could feel 50,000 sets of eyes burning through his skin"?

    A) The 50,000 people in the stadium were trying to hurt Alfie.

    B) Alfie felt uncomfortable and exposed in front of my so many people.

    C) Alfie felt immense pressure from the 50,000 people watching him.

    D) The people in the stadium are warning Alfie that the field is on fire.

82. Which of the following indicates the beginning of a sequence?

    A) Although she was initially apprehensive about the class, she soon grew to enjoy it.

    B) Before he decided what to order for dinner, he had to decide on a restaurant.

    C) At the moment, I can think of nothing more wonderful than a glass of lemonade.

    D) To begin the restoration, they tore out the rotten floorboards.

83. Which of the following best describes the mode of the passage?

    A) expository

    B) narrative

    C) persuasive

    D) descriptive

84. Start with the shapes shown below. Follow the directions.

    1.   Move triangle 1 to the right of triangle 3.

    2.   Swap triangles 2 and 3.

    3.   Rotate triangle 6 180 degrees.

    4.   Swap triangles 4 and 1.

Which of the following shows the order in which the shapes now appear?

    A)

    B)

    C)

    D)

The next two questions are based on this passage.

> Hannah —
>
> Congratulations on the promotion! I just heard the news from the receptionist in Accounting—she says you're already packing up to move into your big new office.
>
> Before you make the official move to upper management, I'd like to make sure we get proper documentation in place for your replacement. (You remember what a pain it was when you trained a few years ago.) To that end, could you please make a list of your current job responsibilities and include a list of all currently available training material that will be necessary for the person who takes over that job? If you feel new training documents are necessary, please include a description of these, and I'll have someone type them up for you.
>
> Congratulations again—you've earned it.
>
> Best regards,
>
> Sasha

85. Which of the following best captures the author's purpose?

A) to inform Hannah that the receptionist in Accounting is telling people about her promotion

B) to let Hannah know she has performed well at work despite not receiving good training

C) to congratulate Hannah on her promotion

D) to acquire information from Hannah in order to train her replacement

86. Which of the following best describes the relationship of the writer to Hannah?

A) Hannah's manager

B) Hannah's coworker

C) Hannah's friend

D) Hannah's replacement

The next two questions are based on the passage below.

East River High School has released its graduation summary for the class of 2016. Out of a total of 558 senior students, 525 (94 percent) successfully completed their degree program and graduated. Of these, 402 (representing 72 percent of the total class) went on to attend to a two- or four-year college or university. The distribution of students among the four main types of colleges and universities—small or large private and small or large public—is shown in the corresponding figure. As the data shows, the majority of East River High School's college-attending graduates chose a large, public institution.

87. According to the figure, how many students from East River High School will attend a small, public college or university?

A) 4

B) 44

C) 440

D) 4400

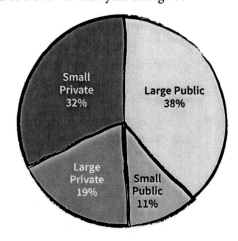

88. Which of the following best describes the tone of the passage?

A) professional

B) casual

C) concerned

D) congratulatory

89. A man is examining cake recipes to find one that will be suitable for his friend, who cannot eat dairy products. According the lists of required ingredients, which of the following should he choose?

A) Recipe Ingredients – flour, sugar, water, milk, eggs, baking powder, baking soda, chocolate powder, almonds

B) Recipe Ingredients – cake flour, vegetable oil, butter, eggs, baking powder, chocolate chips

C) Recipe Ingredients – flour, brown sugar, butter, eggs, baking soda, vanilla extract, macadamia nuts

D) Recipe Ingredients – flour, sugar, brown sugar, vegetable oil, eggs, applesauce, baking powder, vanilla extract

90. A student has written the paragraph below as an introduction to a paper. Which of the following is most likely the topic of the paper?

It has now been two decades since the introduction of thermonuclear fusion weapons into the military inventories of the great powers, and more than a decade since the United States, Great Britain, and the Soviet Union ceased to test nuclear weapons in the atmosphere. Today our understanding of the technology of thermonuclear weapons seems highly advanced, but our knowledge of the physical and biological consequences of nuclear war is continuously evolving.

United States Arms Control and Disarmament Agency, Worldwide Effects of Nuclear War: Some Perspectives, 1998

A) the impact of thermonuclear weapons on the military

B) the technology of thermonuclear weapons

C) atmospheric testing of nuclear weapons

D) the physical and biological consequences of nuclear war

The next two questions are based on this passage.

Ms. Rodriguez —

A recent review of our accounts has shown that you were mistakenly overcharged for your October water bill. Due to a system error, customers in your area were charged twice for their October water usage. We regret the error, and are currently in the process of issuing refunds using the following criteria:

- Customers who paid with a debit card or bank account will receive refunds directly deposited into their bank accounts.
- Credit card transactions will be canceled by our company and will not appear on your statement.
- Customer who paid via check will receive a refund check in the mail in 4 – 6 weeks.

Your business is important to us, and we value your continued support. To demonstrate our commitment to our customers, we will be offering a 5% discount during the month of November to customers affected by this accounting error.

Please contact me directly if you have any questions about your bill or the refund process.

Regards,

Timothy Halgren

Director, Customer Relations

Greenway Water Company

91. Which of the following best describes the purpose of the passage?

A) to inform customers that they will receive a 5% discount on their water bills during the month of November

B) to inform customers that they were overcharged and will be receiving refunds

C) to urge customers to contact their customer service representatives with questions about their bills

D) to thank customers for their continued support

92. Which of the following conclusions is well supported by the passage?

A) Greenway Water Company will soon go out of business when customers leave.

B) Ms. Rodriguez will receive a refund check in the mail in 4 – 6 weeks.

C) Greenway Water Company is concerned that customers may be upset by the error.

D) All customers of Greenway Water Company will receive refunds for being overcharged in October.

The next two questions are based on the index below.

New Zealand .... 125 – 127, 212 – 215, 306

Nicaragua.. 76, 132 – 151

Niger.. 15 – 22, 317 – 320

Nigeria ....16 – 18, 246

North Korea ....101 – 105, 221 – 231, 313

Norway.. 135 – 140, 295

93. A student wants to find information on the Oslo, the capital of Norway. According the index for a geography book, where should the student look first?

A) 15

B) 125

C) 135

D) 221

94. A student wants to find information on rivers in Niger. According the index for a geography book, where should the student look first?

A) 15

B) 101

C) 212

D) 313

The next three questions are based on this passage.

We've been told for years that the recipe for weight loss is fewer calories in than calories out. In other words, eat less and exercise more, and your body will take care of the rest. As many of those who've tried to diet can attest, this edict doesn't always produce results. If you're one of those folks, you might have felt that you just weren't doing it right—that the failure was all your fault.

However, several new studies released this year have suggested that it might not be your fault at all. For example, a study of people who'd lost a high percentage of their body weight (>17%) in a short period of time found that they could not physically maintain their new weight. Scientists measured their resting metabolic rate and found that they'd need to consume only a few hundred calories a day to meet their metabolic needs. Basically, their bodies were in starvation mode and seemed to desperately hang on to each and every calorie. Eating even a single healthy, well-balanced meal a day would cause these subjects to start packing back on the pounds.

Other studies have shown that factors like intestinal bacteria, distribution of body fat, and hormone levels can affect the manner in which our bodies process calories. There's also the fact that it's actually quite difficult to measure the number of calories consumed during a particular meal and the number used while exercising.

95. Which of the following would be the best summary statement to conclude the passage?

A) It turns out that conventional dieting wisdom doesn't capture the whole picture of how our bodies function.

B) Still, counting calories and tracking exercise is a good idea if you want to lose weight.

C) In conclusion, it's important to lose weight responsibly: losing too much weight at once can negatively impact the body.

D) It's easy to see that diets don't work, so we should focus less on weight loss and more on overall health.

96. Which of the following type of arguments is used in the passage?

A) emotional argument

B) appeal to authority

C) specific evidence

D) rhetorical questioning

97. Which of the following would weaken the author's argument?

A) a new diet pill from a pharmaceutical company that promises to help patients lose weight by changing intestinal bacteria

B) the personal experience of a man who was able to lose a significant amount of weight taking in fewer calories than he used

C) a study showing that people in different geographic locations lose different amounts of weight when on the same diet

D) a study showing that people often misreport their food intake when part of a scientific study on weight loss

The next two questions are based on this chart.

Table 1.2. Prices of Office Supplies

MANUFACTURER	SHIPPING AND HANDLING
Discount Office Supplies	$0.99 per pound
Paper Clips & Staples	$12.99 flat fee for all packages
Quick & Fast Office Supplies	$7.99 flat fee for all packages under 10 pounds; $1.99 per additional pound
Blanchard Supplies	free shipping on packages under 10 pounds; $15.99 flat fee for all packages over 10 pounds

98. A company is planning ordering office supplies that will weigh 22 pounds. Based on the pricing chart, which of the following manufacturers would offer the lowest cost for shipping and handling?

A) Discount Office Supplies

B) Paper Clips & Staples

C) Quick & Fast Office Supplies

D) Blanchard Supplies

99. A company is placing an order for office supplies that will weigh 11 pounds. Based on the pricing chart, which of the following manufacturers would offer the lowest cost for shipping and handling?

A) Discount Office Supplies

B) Paper Clips & Staples

C) Quick & Fast Office Supplies

D) Blanchard Supplies

The next two questions are based on this passage.

American Cowslip: This plant grows spontaneously in Virginia and other parts of North America. It flowers in the beginning of May, and the seeds ripen in July, soon after which the stalks and leaves decay, so that the roots remain inactive till the following spring. It is propagated by offsets, which the roots put out freely when they are in a loose moist soil and a shady situation; the best time to remove the roots, and take away the offsets, is in August, after the leaves and stalks are decayed, that they may be fixed well in their new situation before the frost comes on.

William Curtis, *The Botanical Magazine*, 1790

100. According to the passage, which of the following is the best time to remove the roots of American Cowslip?

 A) August

 B) May

 C) July

 D) December

101. Which of the following is the meaning of *propagated* as used in the sentence?

 A) killed

 B) multiplied

 C) extracted

 D) concealed

102. Elaine was feeling <u>lethargic</u> after a poor night's sleep, but she still managed to get to work on time.

 Which of the following is the definition of the underlined word in the sentence above?

 A) tired

 B) confused

 C) angry

 D) rushed

103. Which of the following represents the temperature in degrees Fahrenheit according to the thermometer above?

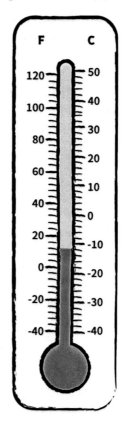

 A) −10

 B) 48

 C) 54

 D) 76

104. Based on the pattern in the headings, which of the following is a reasonable heading to insert in the blank spot?

5. The Human Digestive System
A. The Digestive Tract
1) Mouth
2) Esophagus
3) _____
4) Intestines
B. Accessory Organs
1) Salivary Glands
2) Liver
3) Gall Bladder

A) Stomach

B) Pancreas

C) Heart

D) Proteins

ANSWER KEY

1. **B) is correct.** The purpose of the passage is to explain what an idealist believes in. The author does not offer any opinions or try to persuade readers about the importance of certain values.

2. **D) is correct.** All of these headings describe general types of travel, and road trips fit into this category.

3. **D) is correct.** The loyal dog is presented in contrast with humans, who are not always trustworthy or faithful.

4. **A) is correct.** The author is describing the constancy of dogs as friends. He concludes by stating, "When all other friends desert, he [a dog] remains."

5. **C) is correct.** The passage emphasizes that people can be treacherous, but a dog will be a constant friend. The passage does not suggest that relationships with other people are pointless or useless.

6. **D) is correct.** The author is trying to persuade his audience that dogs are loyal friends.

7. **B) is correct.** The first step in the *After Planting* section is to water the plants immediately.

8. **A) is correct.** In the *Before Planting* section, the directions say to mix in fertilizer or compost after the soil has been loosened.

9. **C) is correct.** The author and Alan have a friendly relationship, as evidenced by the author's casual tone and his offer to bring Alan a gift from his vacation.

10. **C) is correct.** The author is writing to tell Alan that he will be out of the office. The details about his trip and the meeting support this idea.

11. **B) is correct.** The Scout Camp is due north of the Fire Circle.

12. **A) is correct.** The Old Oak Tree lies on the trail between the Fishing Pond and the Fire Circle.

13. **D) is correct.** The author wants to bring customers into Carl's Car Depot, doing so by highlighting the low prices and range of cars available.

14. **B) is correct.** The word *sell* best describes the author's implication that the cars are priced to be sold quickly.

15. **A) is correct.** The passage does not mention warranties.

16. **C) is correct.** The word *said* is italicized to provide emphasis and contrast with the word actions.

17. **A) is correct.** Choice A describes the order of Julia's actions that matches chronological order of the passage.

18. **B) is correct.** The passage describes how Julia had an exhausting morning, and it can be assumed that when "she'd had enough" she decided to go home.

19. **C) is correct.** Whether or not it was irresponsible for Julia to leave work is a matter of opinion. Some readers may agree, and others may disagree. The other statements are facts that can be proven from the passage.

20. **B) is correct.** The phrase "set a course for home" is an idiom that means to head in a certain direction, so Julia is planning to go home.

21. **D) is correct.** The passage emphasizes that Julia is tired, so she's most likely to drive home and go to sleep.

22. **D) is correct.** In the passage, Thomas Jefferson is defined as an anti-Federalist, in contrast with Federalists who believe in a strong federal government.

23. **B) is correct.** *Tropical Frogs* belongs under the heading *Frogs* with the other types of frogs. The blank spot should not include a specific type of frog or refer to amphibians other than frogs.

24. **A) is correct.** Only Choice A is a source produced by someone who does not have first-hand experience of World War I.

25. **A) is correct.** Victoria's win implies that she played in a competitive event.

26. **D) is correct.** Quarter Price Books has the lowest price:
(3.99 × 25) + (2.99 × 50) = 249.25

27. **B) is correct.** The Book Barn would offer the lowest price: $98 for twenty-five books.

28. **A) is correct.** A company that profits from private tutoring might introduce bias into a study on the effects of private tutoring in schools.

29. **C) is correct.** The author cites data from a study to support his or her argument.

30. **C) is correct.** Choice C shows the correct order of the blocks after following the directions.

31. **D) is correct.** Choice D correctly lists the houses the author visited as listed chronologically in the passage.

32. **B) is correct.** The author says that the house on Pine Street "had enough space inside but didn't have a big enough yard for our three dogs."

33. **B) is correct.** A local paper is the source most likely to provide an unbiased assessment of the candidates in a state election.

34. **D) is correct.** The passage concludes with the statement "our Human Resources team will be taking longer than previously stated to review candidates and schedule interviews" and a time window in which Mr. Morgan can expect to receive feedback.

35. **A) is correct.** The author of the passage states that the team will be taking "longer than previously stated," implying that she had previously told Mr. Morgan that the process would take less than two weeks.

36. **C) is correct.** The passage states that babies' senses are much like those of their adult counterparts with the exception of their vision, which develops later.

37. **B) is correct.** The passage states that "infants rely primarily on hearing."

38. **A) is correct.** The passage explains how a baby's senses develop and allow it to interact with the world.

39. **C) is correct.** Ginger appears on the list for fall.

40. **B) is correct.** *Lamb* fits best with the pattern of subheadings naming specific types of meat.

41. **B) is correct.** Only Choice B includes the fact that both Epimetheus and Prometheus were assigned to create living things; it then clarifies that Epimetheus gave positive traits to animals, while Prometheus gave fire to humans. This choice includes all the important parts of the passage without adding other emotions or details.

42. **D) is correct.** The word *given* best describes the idea that the gifts have been handed out.

43. **A) is correct.** Page 55 is included in the section on Italian painters.

44. **C) is correct.** Page 153 is the beginning of the section on High Renaissance architecture, which includes the year 1518.

45. **B) is correct.** In February the service earned $1100, and in April it earned $200. The difference between the two months is $900.

46. **B) is correct.** The author uses several markers of casual writing, including the first person, exclamation marks, and informal language.

47. **D) is correct.** The passage states that restaurateurs must be "exact and ruthless with their budget and pricing." The success of The Hot Dog implies that its owners have done that.

48. **D) is correct.** *Evidence* best describes the idea that The Hot Dog's longevity is proof of its owners' skills.

49. **C) is correct.** The transition word *finally* indicates that it is the end of a sequence.

50. **B) is correct.** While the bold words are adverbs, their purpose is to emphasize the words they describe.

51. **A) is correct.** The index shows that the Battle of the Scheldt appears on page 110.

52. **D) is correct.** The passage describes human studies as the study of "the relationship between human activity and the environment," which would include farmers interacting with river systems.

53. **A) is correct.** The passage explains what the study of geography involves and outlines its main sub-disciplines.

54. **B) is correct.** Only this choice summarizes the two main points of the passage: the definition of geography and the breakdown of its sub-disciplines.

55. **A) is correct.** The raffle is the only feature described as an event the organizers will be "bringing back."

56. **C) is correct.** The "record number of visitors" is the highest, or best, number of visitors to the fair.

57. **C) is correct.** The passage is trying to persuade people to attend the Friendswood Village Summer Fair.

58. **A) is correct.** Only "Facial Expressions" fits with the other subheadings under the category "Involuntary Physical Symptoms of Emotion."

59. **A) is correct.** Only *Green Tea* fits the pattern of headings that describe categories of tea based on color.

60. **A) is correct.** Page 155 is included in the section that covers the end of World War II.

61. **C) is correct.** Page 311 is included in the section on depictions of the Cold War in popular culture between 1945 and 1991.

62. **B) is correct.** The author notes de Tocqueville's observation: "The more I advanced in the study of American society, the more I perceived that the equality of conditions is the fundamental fact from which all others seem to be derived," implying that equality was the most important ideal in the United States.

63. **A) is correct.** *New* best describes the idea that the writer is encountering things he has never seen before.

64. **D) is correct.** "Equality of conditions" suggests that people's living conditions, in terms of economics and social status, were equal.

65. **B) is correct.** Letters from a first-hand witness would be a primary source.

66. **B) is correct.** The word *conquistadors* is italicized to indicate it is in a foreign language.

67. **B) is correct.** The fact that the light is affecting how a painting is viewed implies that the word light is being used to describe the electromagnetic waves that make human vision possible.

68. **C) is correct.** Of the four choices, only Sycamore Apartments is located on Main Street south of the train station.

69. **B) is correct.** The scale shows that the two buildings are approximately 1 mile apart.

70. **D) is correct.** This choice lists the steps for brewing coffee in the same order as the passage.

71. **B) is correct.** The writer uses the first person, showing his or her opinion, to recommend a French press as the best way to brew coffee.

72. **A) is correct.** The author describes the steps for making coffee in chronological order.

73. **D) is correct.** The passage mentions several times that decisions about things like water minerals, ground size, and steep time will depend on the preference of the coffee drinker.

74. **A) is correct.** The passage as a whole describes from start to finish how to make a cup of coffee the drinker will enjoy.

75. **A) is correct.** The author argues that "every man, woman and child should learn" to swim, and then explains to the reader why he or she should be able to swim.

76. **D) is correct.** The author wants to persuade the reader that swimming is a necessary skill.

77. **C) is correct.** *Misuse* best describes the passage's implication that student ID cards have been used incorrectly or fraudulently.

78. **B) is correct.** The new policy states that the "student must apply for a replacement ID card in person at the Student Admissions Office. Online applications will no longer be accepted."

79. **B) is correct.** As shown in the title and opening sentence, the passage is written to inform students about changes to the policy.

80. **C) is correct.** The crowd's support for Alfie and their collective roar after the shot implies that Alfie scored the goal and won the championship.

81. **C) is correct.** The metaphor implies that Alfie felt pressure from the people watching him to perform well. There is no indication that he is threatened physically.

82. **D) is correct.** This statement starts with the phrase *to begin*, which introduces a series or sequence.

83. **B) is correct.** The passage is narrative, meaning it tells a story.

84. **A) is correct.** Choice A shows the correct order and placement of the triangles after following the directions.

85. **D) is correct.** While the passage opens with a congratulatory message, the main purpose of the passage is to ask for a list of job responsibilities and training materials from Hannah.

86. **B) is correct.** The tone and content of the passage implies that the writer is a coworker of Hannah's. She is likely not her manager, since she just learned of the promotion. She is also not the replacement, since she is planning to train that person in the future.

87. **B) is correct.** The passage states that 402 students went on to attend college or university, and 11 percent of 402 is approximately 44 students.

88. **A) is correct.** The passage is written in a neutral, professional tone. It does not include any informal, emotional, or first-person language.

89. **D) is correct.** Only this recipe does not include milk or butter, both of which are dairy products.

90. **D) is correct.** The passage gives a short history of thermonuclear weapons and then introduces its main topic—the physical and biological consequences of nuclear war.

91. **B) is correct.** The main purpose of the passage is to inform customers about the accounting error and to let them know how they will receive their refunds.

92. **C) is correct.** The company ends the passage by expressing its appreciation for customers and offering both a discount and a personal contact within the company, implying it is trying to improve customer relations.

93. **C) is correct.** The index shows that page 135 is the first mention of Norway in the book.

94. **A) is correct.** The index shows that page 15 is the first mention of Niger in the book.

95. **A) is correct.** The bulk of the passage is dedicated to showing that conventional wisdom about "fewer calories in than calories out" isn't true for many people and is more complicated than previously believed.

96. **C) is correct.** The author cites several scientific studies to support the argument.

97. **D) is correct.** People misreporting the amount of food they ate would introduce error into studies on weight loss and might make the studies the author cites unreliable.

98. **B) is correct.** Paper Clips & Staples offers the cheapest shipping and handling cost for a 22-pound package.

99. **C) is correct.** Quick & Fast Office Supplies offers the cheapest shipping and handling cost for an 11-pound package: $7.99 + (1.99 \times 1) = \$9.98$.

100. **A) is correct.** The passage states that "the best time to remove the roots, and take away the offsets, is in August."

101. **B) is correct.** *Multiplied* best describes the passage's description of how the plant reproduces by producing offsets.

102. **A) is correct.** The context of the sentence of having a poor night's sleep indicates that Elaine must be feeling tired.

103. **C) is correct.** 12 degrees F (Fahrenheit) corresponds to 54 degrees C (Celsius) on the thermometer's scale.

104. **A) is correct.** The stomach is the only choice that is an organ in the human digestive tract.

SCIENCE

Directions: Read the question carefully, and choose the best answer.

1. What is the basic unit of volume in the metric system?

   A. meter

   B. milliliter

   C. liter

   D. gram

2. What is the field of geology primarily concerned with?

   A. the Earth

   B. volcanos

   C. the sky

   D. the moon

3. What is chemistry?

   A. study of chemical elements

   B. study of the earth

   C. study of the planets

   D. the study of life

4. What is one method to convert the Celsius scale to the Fahrenheit scale?

   A. $C = F + 32$

   B. $C = 32 + \left(\frac{9}{5}\right)F$

   C. $F = 32 + C\left(\frac{5}{9}\right)$

   D. $C = 95 \times F$

5. There are two primarily building blocks which are used by plants during photosynthesis in order to make sugars (primarily glucose). What are they?

   A. water and carbon dioxide

   B. dirt and air

   C. nitrogen and carbon

   D. water and oxygen

6. The outermost part of a cell is known as the plasma membrane. What is the plasma membrane called in plants and bacteria (and some fungi)?

   A. plasma membrane

   B. permeable membrane

   C. cell wall

   D. mosaic membrane

7. The process of cell division which results in two daughter cells with the same number of chromosomes as the parent cell is _____.

   A. mitosis

   B. division

   C. meiosis

   D. sex

8. What is the fundamental biological unit that is used in order to build protein structures?

   A. nucleic acids

   B. amino acids

   C. elements

   D. water

9. What is the organ of the human body which helps to pump blood throughout the circulatory system?

   A. lungs

   B. heart

   C. hemoglobin

   D. brain

10. In 1 inch, there are 2.54 centimeters. In 1 foot, there are 12 inches. How many centimeters are there in 1 foot?

    A. 30.48

    B. 10.43

    C. 12

    D. 24.5

11. Which organ is the location at which circulating blood is oxygenated in order to carry oxygen to the tissues of the body?

    A. brain

    B. heart

    C. lungs

    D. skin

12. What is absolute zero?

    A. 0°C

    B. 0 Kelvin

    C. −32°C

    D. 0°F

13. What organ system contains your skin?

    A. the respiratory system

    B. the epithelial system

    C. the lymphatic system

    D. the circulatory system

14. Which kind of subatomic particle is found outside of the nucleus (and carries a negative charge)?

    A. electronino

    B. neutron

    C. proton

    D. electron

15. Which subatomic particle is used to determine the atomic number of an element?

    A. neutron

    B. proton

    C. neutrino

    D. electron

16. What is the term that is primarily used for a gene which will be expressed even when a different allele is present?

    A. pragmatic

    B. recessive

    C. dominant

    D. denim

17. _____ is the process through which cells convert the nutrients that they received into ATP.

    A. cellular respiration

    B. diffusion

    C. permeability

    D. nuclear splitting

18. What is the primary difference between a cell membrane and a cell wall?

    A. A cell membrane is flexible, and a cell wall is rigid.

    B. A cell membrane is not found in plants, whereas a cell wall is.

    C. A cell membrane is not found in animals, whereas a cell wall is.

    D. A cell membrane is composed of protein, whereas a cell wall is composed of sugar.

19. What is the highest (broadest) level of classification in biology?

A. phylum

B. species

C. class

D. kingdom

20. What is the first element on the periodic table?

A. plutonium

B. iron

C. hydrogen

D. helium

21. What color of light is not used by the leaves of most plants?

A. red

B. blue

C. violet

D. green

22. What is the definition of force?

A. weight due to gravity

B. the color of an object

C. speed across a distance

D. interaction resulting in a change of motion

23. What type of energy is used by plants during the process of photosynthesis in order to assist in making sugar?

A. moonlight

B. sunlight

C. electricity

D. friction

24. What is the study of physics concerned with?

A. matter and its motion

B. chemical substances

C. life processes

D. telekinesis

25. _____ is a term which is used to describe the changes in organisms over a period of time in terms of their traits and genes.

A. chemistry

B. biology

C. evolution

D. astronomy

26. What is the basic unit of distance in the metric system?

A. liter

B. meter

C. gram

D. centimeter

27. What is genetic drift?

A. when a group of individuals leaves a large population and becomes genetically different over time

B. when genes float through the bloodstream

C. when seeds float on air currents

D. when biological "rafts" carry cells to new locations

28. Which of the following is not in the Kingdom Plantae?

A. cactus

B. algae

C. oak Tree

D. sunflower

29. Upon touching a chair cushion and then a metal plate, John notices that the metal plate feels much colder than the cushion, although the surrounding air temperature is the same. What is an explanation for this?

A. The chair cushion has a higher heat capacity than the metal plate.

B. The metal plate has a higher heat transfer rate than the chair cushion.

C. The metal plate is able to absorb more heat from the air than the cushion.

D. The chair cushion produces some internal heat.

30. Plants are autotrophs, meaning that they:

   A. consume organic material produced by animals

   B. produce their own food

   C. are able to move by themselves

   D. can automatically transform from a seed into a plant

31. Which of the following is not true of a virus?

   A. Viruses have DNA.

   B. Viruses do not have a nucleus.

   C. Viruses cannot survive without water.

   D. Viruses can be infectious.

32. In the digestive system, the majority of nutrients are absorbed in the:

   A. esophagus

   B. stomach

   C. small Intestine

   D. large Intestine

33. How many pairs of human chromosomes exist?

   A. 17

   B. 13

   C. 23

   D. 29

34. Animals engaging in a symbiotic relationship will do which of the following?

   A. help each other survive

   B. take one another's food

   C. attack one another

   D. eat each other

35. If a gene is expressed, then that means that:

   A. It is influencing a phenotype trait.

   B. It is being copied into another set of DNA.

   C. It will be passed on from mother to son.

   D. The gene will produce some hormones.

36. Which of the following structures is found in eukaryotes but not in prokaryotes?

   A. a cell wall

   B. mitochondria

   C. a nuclear membrane

   D. vacuoles

37. If a pitcher throws a baseball into the air and notices that it takes 5 seconds to reach its peak, how long will the baseball need to fall back to the ground? Neglect air resistance.

   A. 2.5 seconds

   B. 9.8 seconds

   C. 5.0 seconds

   D. 10.0 seconds

38. Which of the following is correct regarding an aqueous substance?

   A. It is soluble in water.

   B. It is very reactive.

   C. It is soluble in hydrocarbon.

   D. It is able to dissolve most other compounds.

39. In order for work to be performed, a force has to be:

   A. applied to an object

   B. applied to a surface

   C. applied to a moving object

   D. applied over a distance to an object.

40. One of the primary differences between fungi and plants is that:

   A. Fungi can produce their own food and plants cannot.

   B. Plants have chlorophyll and fungi do not.

   C. Fungi are able to grow without water and plants cannot.

   D. Fungi and plants have no major differences.

41. During which of the following geologic periods did the majority of life develop?

A. Triassic

B. Permian

C. Cretaceous

D. Cambrian

42. The nearest star to the sun is about 4.2 light-years away and is known as:

A. Alpha Centauri

B. Barnard's Star

C. Sirius A

D. Proxima Centauri

43. A mutation in DNA can be caused by all of the following except:

A. ultraviolet radiation

B. chemical exposure

C. DNA replication error

D. exonic duplication

44. People who suffer from Type I diabetes are lacking function in which organ?

A. liver

B. pancreas

C. stomach

D. heart

45. Which of the following organisms is capable of asexual reproduction?

A. squash plant

B. amoeba

C. salmon

D. koala bear

46. In our atmosphere, nitrogen is the most common element, and makes up approximately what percentage?

A. 25%

B. 51%

C. 65%

D. 78%

47. In the human body, which of the following is responsible for clotting blood?

A. platelets

B. white blood cells

C. red blood cells

D. osteoplasts

48. In plants, the female reproductive structures reside in the pistil, whereas the male reproductive structures are in the:

A. stamen

B. anther

C. sepals

D. petals

49. In the human body, communication occurring from cell to cell can happen through the use of:

A. neurotransmitters

B. pili

C. flagella

D. ATP

50. In the following list, which would be considered to be at the top of the food chain?

A. snake

B. mouse

C. hawk

D. tomato plant

51. Tundra, rainforest, and prairie are all examples of ecological classifications known as:

A. ecomes

B. partitions

C. biomes

D. communities

52. According to electron theory, what is the maximum number of bonds a carbon atom can have?

   A. two

   B. three

   C. four

   D. five

53. If a rowboat weighs 50 kilograms, how much water needs to be displaced in order for the boat to float?

   A. 25 liters

   B. 50 liters

   C. 100 liters

   D. 500 liters

54. Given the reaction: $CaSO_{4(aq)} + CuCl_{2(aq)} \rightarrow$, which of the following is a possible product?

   A. CaCl

   B. CaCu

   C. $CuSO_3$

   D. $CaCl_2$

55. A ball with a mass of 0.5 kg is moving at 10 m/s. How much kinetic energy does it have?

   A. 15 Joules

   B. 25 Joules

   C. 50 Joules

   D. 55.5 Joules

56. Testes are an organ found in:

   A. females

   B. plants

   C. males

   D. amoebas

57. How many kingdoms of life are there?

   A. three

   B. six

   C. seven

   D. nine

58. A volcano that is low and flat to the ground, and does not typically have large, violent eruptions can be classified as what?

   A. a plane volcano

   B. a cinder cone

   C. a shield volcano

   D. a screen volcano

59. Which of these types of rocks is created near or on the earth's surface?

   A. igneous rock

   B. sedimentary rock

   C. crustaceous rock

   D. metamorphic rock

60. Which of the following is true regarding deoxyribonucleic acid (DNA). in the human body?

   A. DNA is used as an energy source.

   B. DNA is used as a template for creation of proteins.

   C. DNA is only found in the brain.

   D. DNA is made of sugar.

61. Which of the following is *not* present in an animal cell?

   A. nucleus

   B. mitochondria

   C. cytoplasm

   D. cell wall

62. Which of the following is not an organ system in humans?

   A. the endocrine system

   B. the respiratory system

   C. the exophytic system

   D. the muscular system

63. The age of the Earth is closest to:

   A. 100 million years

   B. 1.2 billion years

   C. 4.5 billion years

   D. 25.0 billion years

64. Plants absorb carbon dioxide (CO_2) to create sugar for energy. What is the primary byproduct of this process?

    A. oxygen

    B. nitrogen

    C. carbon monoxide

    D. carbon

65. According to Newton's first law, $F = M \times A$, how fast will a 10-kilogram object accelerate when pushed with 50 Newtons of force?

    A. 2.5 m/s^2

    B. 5.0 m/s^2

    C. 8.0 m/s^2

    D. 15.0 m/s^2

66. What prevents ultraviolet radiation produced by the sun from damaging life on earth?

    A. the ozone layer

    B. greenhouse gasses

    C. the vacuum between earth and the sun

    D. the water layer

67. Mitosis is the process of cell division to create new cells. What is the process of cell division required to create new sex cells or gametes?

    A. teloses

    B. meiosis

    C. kinesis

    D. phoresis

68. What are the two main parts of the human body's central nervous system?

    A. the heart and the spinal cord

    B. the brain and the spinal cord

    C. the peripheral nerves and the brain

    D. the spinal cord and the peripheral nerves

69. Humans can turn glucose into ATP, the basic energy molecule in the body. What is a byproduct of this process?

    A. carbon dioxide

    B. oxygen

    C. nitrogen

    D. phosphorus

70. What is true of elements found in the same group (column) in the periodic table?

    A. They have the same atomic mass.

    B. They have the same level of reactivity.

    C. They have the same number of protons.

    D. The have the same number of valence electrons.

71. Compounds that are acidic will be able to lower the pH of a solution, by doing which of the following?

    A. accepting H+ ions

    B. releasing H+ ions

    C. binding with acidic species in solution

    D. reducing oxidative species in solution

72. Which of the following elements is the most electronegative?

    A. chlorine

    B. iron

    C. magnesium

    D. silicon

73. How did mountains on the earth's surface primarily form?

    A. through the shifting of tectonic plates

    B. through the impact of meteors

    C. through gradual erosion

    D. through accumulation of soil by the wind

ANSWER KEY

1.	C.	**18.**	C.	**39.**	D.	**56.**	C.
2.	A.	**19.**	D.	**44.**	B.	**57.**	B.
5.	A.	**20.**	D.	**40.**	D.	**58.**	B.
9.	B.	**21.**	B.	**41.**	D.	**63.**	D.
3.	D.	**22.**	A.	**42.**	D.	**66.**	C.
8.	C.	**23.**	C.	**43.**	B.	**73.**	C.
13.	A.	**24.**	B.	**45.**	B.	**61.**	A.
4.	B.	**25.**	A.	**46.**	D.	**71.**	B.
6.	B.	**26.**	B.	**47.**	A.	**62.**	A.
7.	A.	**36.**	B.	**48.**	B.	**64.**	B.
10.	C.	**28.**	B.	**49.**	A.	**65.**	B.
12.	B.	**29.**	C.	**50.**	C.	**67.**	A.
33.	B.	**30.**	C.	**51.**	C.	**68.**	D.
11.	D.	**31.**	C.	**52.**	C.	**69.**	B.
14.	B.	**32.**	A.	**53.**	B.	**70.**	A.
15.	C.	**34.**	A.	**54.**	D.	**72.**	A.
16.	A.	**35.**	C.	**55.**	B.		
27.	A.	**37.**	C.	**59.**	C.		
17.	D.	**38.**	A.	**60.**	B.		

4

WRITING

Directions: Read the question carefully, and choose the best answer.

1. Which of the following sentences follows the rules of capitalization?

   A) As juveniles, african white-backed vultures are darkly colored, developing their white feathers only as they grow into adulthood.

   B) Ukrainians celebrate a holiday called *Malanka* during which men dress in costumes and masks and play tricks on their neighbors.

   C) Because of its distance from the sun, the planet neptune has seasons that last the equivalent of forty-one earth years.

   D) Edward Jenner, considered the Father of immunology, invented the world's first vaccine.

2. Sandra's principal reason for choosing the job was that it would be full-time and would offer benefits.

   Which of the following is the complete subject in the sentence?

   A) Sandra's principal reason for choosing the job

   B) Sandra's principal reason

   C) Sandra's principal

   D) Sandra

3. James had already been awake for nineteen hours___ after a twelve-hour work day, when he received the news.

   A) .

   B) ;

   C) ,

   D) —

4. First and foremost, they receive an <u>annual pension payment. The amount of the pension</u> has been reviewed and changed a number of times, most recently to reflect the salary of a high-level government executive.

   Which of the following would NOT be an acceptable way to revise and combine the underlined portion of the sentences above?

   A) annual pension payment, the amount of which

   B) annual pension payment; the amount of the pension

   C) annual pension payment; over the years since 1958, the amount of the pension

   D) annual pension payment, the amount of the pension

5. Which of the following sentences has the correct subject-verb agreement?

   A) The Akhal-Teke horse breed, originally from Turkmenistan, have long enjoyed a reputation for bravery and fortitude.

   B) The employer decided that he could not, due to the high cost of healthcare, afford to offer other benefits to his employees.

   C) Though Puerto Rico is known popularly for its beaches, its landscape also include mountains, which play home to many of the island's rural villages.

   D) Each of the storm chasers decide whether or not to go out when rain makes visibility low.

6. Which of the following is a compound sentence?

   A) Plague, generally not a major public health concern, actually continues to spread among rodent populations today, and it even occasionally makes its way into a human host.

   B) Modern archeology, which seeks answers to humanity's questions about its past, is helped significantly by new technologies.

   C) In the fight against obesity, countries around the world are imposing taxes on sodas and other sugary drinks in an effort to curb unhealthy habits.

   D) Because the assassination of President John F. Kennedy continues to haunt and fascinate Americans, new movies, books, and television series about it are being released every year.

7. Parrots, among the most intelligent birds in the world, have been prized pets for many centuries; in fact, the first recorded instance of parrot training was written in the thirteenth century.

   Which of the following is a synonym for *prized* as used in the sentence?

   A) unlikely

   B) misunderstood

   C) rewarded

   D) valued

8. Which of the following would most likely be found in an academic research paper on the world's food supply?

   A) It's ridiculous that so many people in the world are hungry while others just throw away tons of uneaten food.

   B) I've always believed that it's our moral duty as a people to provide food and clean water to those who do not have access to it, which is why I have made research of the food supply my life's work.

   C) Advances in agricultural technology over the past five decades have led to a steady increase in the global food supply, and the populations of many countries around the world are benefitting.

   D) Poor people should appeal to their governments for help feeding their families.

9. Which of the following prefixes would be used to indicate that something is *inside* or *within*?

   A) intra–

   B) trans–

   C) anti–

   D) hyper–

10. Which of the following is correctly punctuated?

   A) The artist Prince, whose death shocked America in April of 2016; was one of the most successful musical artists of the last century.

   B) The artist Prince, whose death shocked America in April of 2016, was one of the most successful musical artists of the last century.

   C) The artist Prince—whose death shocked America in April of 2016, was one of the most successful musical artists of the last century.

   D) The artist Prince, whose death shocked America in April of 2016: was one of the most successful musical artists of the last century.

11. Everyday items like potatos, bread, onions, and even saliva are the tools of art conservators, who work to clean and restore works of art.

Which of the following is misspelled in the sentence above?

A) potatos

B) saliva

C) conservators

D) restore

12. Today, astrophysicists study the same stars that were observed by the astronemers of the ancient world, though today's techniques and technology are much more advanced.

Which of the following is misspelled in the sentence?

A) astrophysicists

B) astronemers

C) techniques

D) technology

13. Which of the following nouns is written in the correct plural form?

A) vertebraes

B) gooses

C) octopusses

D) bronchi

14. Which of the following sentences is irrelevant as part of a paragraph composed of these sentences?

A) Traffic around the arena was heavy, so we were worried we'd miss the opening pitch.

B) My brother and I won tickets in a radio station contest to see his favorite team play on opening day.

C) To win the contest, you had to be the 395th caller and know the answer to a trivia question; we waited anxiously by the phone for the contest to begin.

D) My brother has followed the team since childhood, so we knew he'd be able to answer the trivia question correctly.

15. The American Academy of Arts and Sciences includes members whose topics of study span many disciplines such as math, science, arts, humanities, public affairs, and business.

Which of the following is an appropriate synonym for *disciplines* as it is used in the sentence?

A) locations

B) regions

C) punishments

D) fields

16. Which of the following is a complex sentence?

A) When skywriting, a pilot flies a small aircraft in specific, particular formations, creating large letters visible from the ground.

B) The public defense attorney was able to maintain her optimism despite her dearth of courtroom wins, her lack of free time, and her growing list of clients.

C) Because the distance between stars in the galaxy is far greater than the distance between planets, interstellar travel is expected to be an even bigger challenge than interplanetary exploration.

D) Invented in France in the early nineteenth century, the stethoscope underwent a number of reiterations before the emergence of the modern form of the instrument in the 1850s.

17. Unlike a traditional comic book, a graphic novel is released as one single publication, either in the form of one long story or in the form of an anthology.

Which of the following is an appropriate synonym for *traditional* as it is used in the sentence?

A) old-fashioned

B) conventional

C) expensive

D) popular

18. Which of the following statements is true regarding the outline?

1. Types of Engines
A.   Heat engines
i) Combustion engines
ii) Non-combustion heat engines
B.   Electric engines
C.   Physically powered motors
i) Pneumatic motors
ii) Hydraulic motors

A) Heat engines are the most common type of engine.

B) Pneumatic and hydraulic motors are both types of electric engines.

C) The three types of engines are heat engines, electric engines, and pneumatic motors.

D) Heat engines can be broken down into combustion and non-combustion engines.

19. The patient's preoperative evaluation is scheduled for next Wednesday.

In the sentence, the prefix *pre–* indicates that the evaluation will take place at which of the following times?

A) before the operation

B) after the operation

C) during the operation

D) at the end of the operation

20. Which of the following root words would be used in a word related to the body?

A) corp

B) auto

C) man

D) bio

21. Her new tennis racket cost her a hundred bucks, but it was worth the steep price tag.

Which of the following words from the sentence is slang?

A) cost

B) bucks

C) steep

D) tag

22. Though professional dental care is widely available in the developed world, the prevalence of cavities is much higher there.

Which of the following parts of speech is *widely* as used in the sentence?

A) adjective

B) noun

C) adverb

D) verb

23. Typically, water that has evaporated remains in the sky in cloud form for less than ten days before falling to Earth again as precipitation.

Which of the following parts of speech is *remains* as used in the sentence?

A) noun

B) verb

C) adjective

D) adverb

24. Though the term *nomad* is often associated with early populations, nomadic cultures exist today, especially in the mountain's of Europe and Asia.

Which of the following punctuation marks is used incorrectly?

A) the comma after *populations*

B) the comma after *today*

C) the apostrophe in *mountain's*

D) the period after *Asia*

25. On Parents' Day, a public holiday in the Democratic Republic of Congo, families celebrate parents' both living and deceased.

Which of the following punctuation marks is used incorrectly?

A) the apostrophe in *Parents' Day*

B) the comma following *Day*

C) the comma following *Congo*

D) the apostrophe in *parents'*

26. Unfortunately, the belief that changelings could be convinced to leave was not just <u>an innocuous superstition. On some occasions,</u> harm came to the individual who was thought to be a changeling.

Which is the best way to revise and combine the underlined portion of the sentences?

A) an innocuous superstition, on some occasions,

B) an innocuous superstition, but on some occasions,

C) an innocuous superstition; however, on some occasions,

D) an innocuous superstition: on some occasions,

27. Which of the following phrases follows the rules of capitalization?

A) President Carter and his advisors

B) Robert Jones, the senior Senator from California

C) my Aunt and Uncle who live out west

D) the party on New Year's eve

28. In 1983, almost twenty years after his death, T.S. Eliot won two Tony Awards for his contributions to the well-loved musical *Cats*.

Cats is italicized for which of the following reasons?

A) to highlight its importance

B) to indicate it is intentionally misspelled

C) because it is the title of a musical

D) because it is in a foreign language

29. Which of the following sentences has correct pronoun-antecedent agreement?

A) The storm, which included three days of rain, was very strong, and they left half the city flooded.

B) Each of the cars needs to be examined for damage by a mechanic; he may need repairs.

C) The number of people who had to evacuate hasn't been confirmed, but it is small.

D) Many people were able to take advantage of shelters, where he or she was kept safe from the storm.

30. The *Chicago Tribune* is famous for many reasons: in 1948, the paper published an erroneous headline about the winner of the Presidential election, and in 1974, it called for President Nixon's resignation.

Which of the following phrases contains an error in capitalization?

A) *Chicago Tribune*

B) the paper

C) Presidential election

D) President Nixon's

31. In the eighteenth century, renowned composer Wolfgang Amadeus Mozart set to music the poetry of a famous, well-known writer who shared his name–Johann Wolfgang von Goethe.

Which of the following punctuation marks correctly completes the sentence?

A) ,

B) :

C) ;

D) ?

CONTINUE

32. Which of the following sentences has the correct subject-verb agreement?

A) The Iris and B. Gerald Cantor Roof Garden, atop the Metropolitan Museum of Art in New York City, offer a remarkable view.

B) The Mammoth-Flint Ridge Cave System, located in central Kentucky inside Mammoth Cave National Park, are the largest cave system in the world.

C) Andy Warhol's paintings, in addition to being the subject of the largest single-artist museum in the United States, are in great demand.

D) The field of child development are concerned with the emotional, psychological, and biological developments of infants and children.

33. Which of the following would most likely be found in a scientific paper on the history of telescopes?

A) Jerry R. Ehman had always encouraged his kids' love of science by taking them camping and star gazing.

B) In 1977, Jerry R. Ehman, using a powerful radio telescope, detected a signal that seemed to come from outside the Earth's atmosphere.

C) I believe that telescopes have the potential to change our understanding of the universe and our place in it.

D) It's really silly to think that telescopes are a new invention.

34. Vivariums, common in elementary school classrooms, are enclosed spaces designed to replicate a particular habitat.

Which of the following is part of the predicate in the sentence?

A) are enclosed spaces

B) vivariums

C) elementary school classrooms

D) common in

35. The Boat Race, a rowing race that has been held almost annually in London, England, since 1856, was infamously interupted in 2012.

Which of the following is misspelled in the sentence?

A) rowing

B) annually

C) infamously

D) interupted

36. The exotic pet trade is a significant concern for enviornmentalists and animal rights advocates around the world.

Which of the following is misspelled in the sentence?

A) significant

B) enviornmentalists

C) rights

D) advocates

37. In baseball today, strict regulations have standardized the design of bats; they used to come in a wide range of shapes, sizes, and weights.

Which of the following is a synonym for *standardized* as used in the sentence?

A) clarified

B) reconciled

C) normalized

D) ignored

38. Which of the following sentences has correct pronoun-antecedent agreement?

A) Animals use estivation to avoid harsh conditions and to help it survive winter.

B) Some species of fish use luminescent lures to trick other fish into moving closer to it.

C) In a parasitic relationship, one species is negatively affected while the other species acquires what they need to survive.

D) Tropical rainforests are made up of many layers, each of which has its own distinct species.

39. Which of the following prefixes would be used to indicate that something is opposite?

    A) fore–

    B) bi–

    C) anti–

    D) trans–

40. Which of the following is an appropriate synonym for *insolent* as it is used in the sentence?

    The students' insolent behavior drove the teacher to punish the class with extra homework.

    A) confusing

    B) disrespectful

    C) delightful

    D) unlikely

41. Which of the following root words would be used in a word related to time?

    A) gram

    B) crypt

    C) chron

    D) mort

42. Which of the following is correctly punctuated?

    A) In addition to the disastrous effects an active volcano can have on it's immediate surroundings, an eruption can also pose a threat to passing aircraft.

    B) In addition to the disastrous effects an active volcano can have on it's immediate surroundings: an eruption can also pose a threat to passing aircraft.

    C) In addition to the disastrous effects an active volcano can have on its immediate surroundings: an eruption can also pose a threat to passing aircraft.

    D) In addition to the disastrous effects an active volcano can have on its immediate surroundings, an eruption can also pose a threat to passing aircraft.

43. Which of the following would be an acceptable way to combine the two clauses?

    A) While these incidents sometimes end in funny or heartwarming stories, at other times they end in fear and destruction.

    B) While these incidents sometimes end in funny or heartwarming stories; at other times they end in fear and destruction.

    C) While these incidents sometimes end in funny or heartwarming stories: at other times they end in fear and destruction.

    D) While these incidents sometimes end in funny or heartwarming stories— at other times they end in fear and destruction.

44. L.L. Zamenhof, an ophthalmologist in the late 1800s, invented a universal language called Esperanto with the goal of advancing international communications and relations.

    Which of the following is an appropriate synonym for *advancing* as it is used in the sentence?

    A) improving

    B) changing

    C) hastening

    D) celebrating

45. Which of the following is a simple sentence?

    A) Although Sacagawea is famous for her role as guide and interpreter for Lewis and Clark, few know about the mystery surrounding her death.

    B) The high death toll at the end of the Civil War was not exclusively due to battle losses; large numbers of soldiers died as a result of poor living conditions.

    C) Self-driving vehicles are just now being introduced on the automotive market, but research into automating vehicle processes began as early as the 1920s.

    D) Freediving is sometimes combined with other underwater activities such as photography, football, hockey, and even target shooting.

46. The distinguished lexicologist had been with the university for many years.

In the sentence, the prefix *lexi–* indicates that the researcher studies which of the following?

A) literature

B) words

C) plants

D) rocks

47. Which of the following is a complex sentence?

A) Engineers designed seat belts to stop the inertia of traveling bodies by applying an opposing force to the driver and passengers during a collision.

B) Hurricanes cost the United States roughly $5 billion per year in damages and have been the cause of almost two million deaths in the last two hundred years.

C) Woodstock appeared in the *Peanuts* comic strips as early as April of 1967, but he was not named until June of 1970, ten months after the famous music festival of the same name, Woodstock.

D) Although organized firefighting groups existed as early as ancient Egyptian times, the first fully state-run brigade was created by Emperor Augustus of Rome.

48. Which of the following sentences is irrelevant as part of a paragraph composed of these sentences?

A) It looks like the weather might force us to move the game to next weekend.

B) Our team will be playing our biggest rival for the last game of the season.

C) The teams play each other every year, and it's a big event for the town.

D) Last year, the mayor closed down Main Street so fans could celebrate together safely.

49. Which of the following parts of speech is *handsome* as it is used in the sentence?

According to Greek mythology, Narcissus was a hunter who was so handsome that he fell in love with his own reflection.

A) noun

B) verb

C) adjective

D) adverb

50. It's a drag to do homework on the weekend, but I won't pass the class if I spend all day watching TV.

Which of the following words from the sentence is slang?

A) homework

B) pass

C) spend

D) drag

51. In many European countries such as, France, Spain, and Italy, hot chocolate is made with real melted chocolate making for a beverage that is thick and rich.

Which of the following punctuation marks is used incorrectly?

A) the comma after "as"

B) the comma after "France"

C) the comma after "Italy"

D) the period after "rich"

52. Which of the following nouns is written in the correct plural form?

A) shelves

B) phenomenons

C) mans

D) deers

53. Abby's travels in Asia provided her the opportunity to try many foods that she would not have been able to try at home in the United States.

Which of the following parts of speech is *travels* as used in the sentence?

A) verb

B) noun

C) adjective

D) adverb

54. Although the Nile River in Africa, passes through eleven countries, it is the main water source of only two of them—Egypt and Sudan.

Which of the following punctuation marks is used incorrectly?

A) the comma after *Africa*

B) the comma after *countries*

C) the em-dash after *them*

D) the period after *Sudan*

55. Spelunking involves much more than adrenaline: enthusiasts dive into unexplored caves <u>to study structures of, take photographs, and create maps of</u> the untouched systems.

Which is the best way to revise the underlined portion of the sentences?

A) to study structures of, take photographs, and create maps of

B) to study structures of, to take photographs, and create maps of

C) to study structures of, taking photographs of, and creating maps of

D) to study structures, take photographs, and create maps of

56. Which of the following statements is true regarding the outline?

1. The Stages of Labor	
A)	First Stage
	A) Early Phase
	B) Active Phase
	C) Transition Phase
B)	Second Stage
	1. Pushing
	2. Fetal Expulsion
C)	Third Stage
D)	Fourth Stage

A) The Fourth Stage of labor is broken down into two phases.

B) The First Stage of labor is the longest.

C) The First Stage of labor is broken into three phases.

D) Pushing and Fetal Expulsion are parts of the Third Stage of labor.

Informational-essay sample-writing prompt

In recent years, catastrophic hurricanes and typhoons around the world have resulted in large-scale destruction and loss of life. However, rapid population growth and the urban development necessary to accommodate the growth have continued in areas vulnerable to storms and flooding, putting millions at risk.

Proponents of urban development in these urbanizing areas say that they are the economic engines of the economy and must be accommodated to keep economic growth high. Opponents insist that development must be curtailed in the interest of public safety, even if that means limiting economic growth by slowing urban development. Is a compromise possible to allow for economic growth even while keeping people safe?

Read the texts below, and write an essay taking a side and defending your perspective on this issue. Use information from both texts in your essay.

While reading the texts, highlight or note important details. Take a few minutes to plan your essay before you start writing, including defining your argument, how you will introduce it, and what the main points will be for each paragraph.

While writing your essay, make sure you include information from both texts, create a well-organized and coherent essay with an introduction, body, and conclusions, provide details from the texts supporting your argument, use complex sentence structure and transitions, and exhibit strong vocabulary and clear wording.

Passage 1

Powerful and often unexpected disruptive weather patterns and storms in recent years around the world like Hurricane Sandy on the United States North Atlantic coast, Typhoon Haiyan in the Philippines, and Cyclone Pam in Vanuatu have caused extreme destruction in these places. Furthermore, rapid population growth and urban development to accommodate it in areas vulnerable to storms and flooding, from the United States Gulf Coast to Southeast Asia and the Indian Subcontinent, is putting millions at risk. Even though these growing centers of population are the economic engines of their economies and accommodate the workforces that drive the economic growth of these industrial powers, development must be curtailed in the interest of public safety. Rapid population growth has not permitted adequate urban planning, and the proliferation of slums means that more lives will be lost in the case of storms or floods. If slowing urban growth means limiting economic growth, so be it: the risks of flooding from unpredictable and violent climate patterns are too great.

Passage 2

It cannot be denied that extreme weather events in the past decade have been damaging to a number of regions. However, the potential of economic growth and urban development to benefit countries, especially those less developed ones, is too important to ignore. While it's true that a number of major industrial urban areas are located in areas vulnerable to storms and flooding, development in these places must continue, and industry must be fostered to ensure economic stability. The economies of the Philippines, Indonesia, Malaysia, and elsewhere in South and Southeast Asia are growing at an unprecedented rate; slowing development now because of the possibility of a storm would destabilize these countries, and millions of poor and working-class people would suffer job losses and lack of opportunities. Furthermore, areas like the Texas Gulf Coast and the New York/New Jersey coastal areas of the United States are essential to the U.S. and even the world economy. Slowing business growth in these areas would damage the global financial and fossil fuel markets; furthermore, the government has no legal recourse to prevent people from moving to these regions, at least in the United States.

ANSWER KEY

1. **B) is correct.** Both *Ukrainians* and *Malanka* must be capitalized; both are proper nouns, and *Ukrainians* begins a sentence.

2. **A) is correct.** The complete subject includes the main noun (*reason*) and all its accompanying modifying phrases.

3. **C) is correct.** The inessential phrase *after a twelve-hour work day* is being set apart from the rest of the sentence by commas.

4. **D) is correct.** This choice creates a comma splice.

5. **B) is correct.** The verb is the singular *afford*, and its subject is the singular *employer*.

6. **A) is correct.** Here, two independent clauses are connected by a comma plus the coordinating conjunction *and*.

7. **D) is correct.** If these intelligent birds have been kept as pets for so long and if people have taken the time to train them, it is most likely that parrots are *valued* animals.

8. **C) is correct.** This choice uses formal language, the third-person perspective, and non-judgmental language.

9. **A) is correct.** The prefix *intra–* means *inside* or *within*.

10. **B) is correct.** The inessential appositive phrase *whose death shocked America in April of 2016* is correctly set apart from the rest of the sentence by commas. Choices A and D create sentence fragments, and Choice C incorrectly pairs an em dash with a comma.

11. **A) is correct.** *Potatos* should be spelled *potatoes*.

12. **B) is correct.** *Astronemers* should be spelled *astronomers*.

13. **D) is correct.** The noun *bronchus* is made plural by changing the *–us* to *–i*.

14. **A) is correct.** This sentence does not relate to the flow of information provided by the other three, which tell the story of the siblings' experience with the radio contest. It only discusses the siblings' experience attending the game itself.

15. **D) is correct.** *Fields* best describes the idea that members study many different areas of knowledge; furthermore, the word *field* may refer to something intangible. There are many topics of study in many *fields*, or disciplines.

16. **C) is correct.** This sentence includes an independent clause (*interstellar travel is expected to be an even bigger challenge than interplanetary exploration*) and a dependent clause (*Because the distance between stars in the galaxy is far greater than the distance between planets*).

17. **B) is correct.** *Conventional* best describes the idea that comic books have an established narrative framework, a main point in the sentence.

18. **D) is correct.** The two subheadings under "Heat Engines" are "Combustion Engines" and "Non-Combustion Engines."

19. **A) is correct.** The prefix *pre–* means *before*.

20. **A) is correct.** The root word *corp* means *body*.

21. **B) is correct.** *Bucks* is a slang term for *dollars*.

22. **C) is correct.** *Widely* is an adverb modifying the adjective *available*.

23. **B) is correct.** *Remains* is a verb in the sentence.

24. **C) is correct.** *Mountain's* is not possessive in this sentence, so it does not require an apostrophe.

25. **D) is correct.** The second *parents* is plural, not possessive, so it does not require an apostrophe.

26. **D) is correct.** The colon correctly signifies that the second clause builds on the first.

27. **A) is correct.** *President* is a title and should be capitalized when it precedes a name.

29. **C) is correct.** The titles of musicals are always italicized.

28. **C) is correct.** *Number* is singular, so it agrees with the singular pronoun *it*.

30. **C) is correct.** *Presidential* is an adjective describing the election and, as such, should not be capitalized.

31. **B) is correct.** The text following the explanation elaborates on what was said in the first part of the sentence, and is not an independent clause, so a colon is needed.

32. **C) is correct.** Subject and verb only agree in Choice C. In Choice A, *Garden* requires a singular verb (*offers*), as does *System* in Choice B (*is*). In Choice D, the subject *field* requires a singular verb (*is*).

33. **B) is correct.** Choice B is written in an academic style. Choice A discusses a topic that isn't relevant to a scientific paper. Choice C inappropriately uses the first person, and Choice D uses informal language (*really silly*).

34. **A) is correct.** The predicate includes the main verb of the sentence.

35. **D) is correct.** *Interupted* should be spelled *interrupted*.

36. **B) is correct.** *Enviornmentalists* should be spelled *environmentalists*.

37. **C) is correct.** *Normalized* best describes the idea the bats are now all the same shape, size, and weight.

38. **D) is correct.** *Each of which* is singular, so it requires the singular pronoun *its*.

39. **C) is correct.** The prefix *anti–* means *opposite* or *against*. *Fore–* means *before*, *bi–* means *two*, and *trans–* means *across*.

40. **B) is correct.** *Disrespectful* best describes the idea that the students were behaving rudely and deserved to be disciplined.

41. **C) is correct.** *Chron* is used in words relating to time (e.g., *chronology*, *synchronize*).

42. **D) is correct.** Here, a comma correctly sets off the introductory phrase;

furthermore, the sentence does not include an apostrophe in the pronoun *its*.

43. **A) is correct.** The first clause is dependent and the second is independent, so they should be joined by a comma.

44. **A) is correct.** *Improving* best conveys the idea described in the sentence that Esperanto was intended to enhance international communication.

45. **D) is correct.** Only Choice D includes a single independent clause with no other clauses.

46. **B) is correct.** The prefix *lexi–* means *related to words*.

47. **D) is correct.** An independent clause (*the fully…of Rome*) is connected with a dependent clause (*Although organized… Egyptian times*) using a comma.

48. **A) is correct.** The other choices all discuss the importance of the game to the town, so Choice A does not belong.

49. **C) is correct.** In the sentence, *handsome* is an adjective describing Narcissus.

50. **D) is correct.** In the sentence, *drag* is used as a slang term that means something is annoying or boring.

51. **A) is correct.** The comma is not needed to separate *such as* from the list it introduces. A comma is needed to separate items in a series (Choice B) and to set apart an introductory phrase (Choice C). The sentence does not convey emotion or ask a question, so a period (Choice D) is appropriate.

52. **A) is correct.** *Shelf* is correctly made plural as *shelves*. *Phenomenons* should be *phenomena*, *mans* should be *men*, and *deers* should be *deer*.

53. **B) is correct.** *Travels* functions as a noun and is the subject of the sentence.

54. **A) is correct.** A comma should never separate a subject (*Nile River*) from its verb (*passes*). Choice B correctly separates the dependent from the independent clause. Choice D correctly ends the sentence.

55. **D) is correct.** Only in this choice do the three phrases have a similar (parallel) structure (verb + direct object).

56. **C) is correct.** The outline shows that the First Stage of labor is broken down into three phases (Early, Active, and Transition).

Informational-essay sample-writing prompt

Violent storms are a huge risk to human life and property; they also have a strong impact on the economy, interfering with economic activity and sometimes damaging infrastructure. However, natural disasters are a fact of life on our planet, and it's impossible for economic development and growth to cease due to the possibility of a powerful storm. Still, rapid urban development is occurring in particularly storm-prone areas in Asia and even in North America, putting millions of people at risk. While the risks of a calamitous storm should never be underestimated, the solution is not to halt migration and slow economic growth, but to encourage investment in urban planning and public safety.

As discussed in Passage 1, centers of population in storm-prone areas in Indonesia, the Philippines, the United States East and Gulf Coasts, and elsewhere are indeed growing; natural resources and urban areas in these places are essential to local and national economies and even the global economy. During this time of change, especially in areas that are newly developing, opportunities for proper urban planning abound. Before growing urban areas get even larger, governments must take action to prevent the proliferation of slums, improve existing infrastructure to meet the needs of growing cities (or develop new infrastructure), and put policies into place for good urban management. Given the importance of these urban and industrial areas, especially for billion-dollar sectors like the oil and gas industry as mentioned in Passage 2, there may even be opportunities for major companies to get involved in sponsoring urban development and safety in the economic zones and cities relevant to their interests around the world.

Furthermore, with economic growth also comes innovation and technology. Today, there are more opportunities than ever to develop products and procedures to ensure safety. From engineering to preparedness to emergency medical treatment, there are a plethora of approaches to storm readiness and flood control. Urban planning can take into account flooding and geographical impediments to emergency response time. There are more products on the market to help families survive for several days without help (for instance, water purifiers and other survival gear). Governments, civic organizations, and NGOs could be involved in emergency preparedness efforts and enlisted to distribute preparedness items during storm seasons, especially to those poor and working people discussed in Passage 2, who are the most likely to be affected and who, according to Passage 1, would most likely be harmed. Using good technology and wise community coordination would ensure that vulnerable workers and their families are as safe as possible during storm season, so that they could benefit year-round from economic growth.

While storms and other natural disasters are and will remain a threat to human life, it's unrealistic to imagine that all economic activity will stop for the sake of safety. Thanks to economic growth and innovation, we can develop planning, technology, policy, and coordination to ensure the safety of communities as they drive the economic growth of those regions affected by major storms. That way, development can continue in as safe an environment as possible.

5

SOCIAL STUDIES

Read the text carefully, and then answer the questions.

The following passage corresponds with questions 1 and 2.

The landmass of the United States doubled in 1803 with the purchase of the Louisiana Territory from France; this territory stretched from modern-day Louisiana on the Gulf of Mexico north through the Rocky Mountains to parts of what are today Montana and Minnesota. Thomas Jefferson, the president who brokered this deal, believed that the continued moral strength of the young nation depended on the availability of farmland and the possibilities of westward expansion. However, the sale of this land was not without controversy: American politicians of the time debated whether it was constitutional or prudent to increase the size of the nation so rapidly, and it's questionable whether France had legally obtained the land from Spain or had the right to sell it at all.

1. Which of the following is true about the Louisiana Purchase?

   A) It involved a transaction between Spain and the United States.

   B) It was universally considered to be a good idea.

   C) It included territory that would become multiple states in the U.S.

   D) It tripled the landmass area of the United States.

2. Based on the information in the passage, which of the following might be a reason for an American politician of 1803 to oppose the Louisiana Purchase?

   A) The Constitution did not stipulate whether the nation could be increased in size so rapidly.

   B) The price per acre of the land included was too high.

   C) Most of the soil in the regions of the Louisiana Territory was not good farmland.

   D) Giving citizens new areas to farm would strengthen the culture of the nation.

Questions 3 and 4 refer to the following cartoon and information:

THE LAST FEW BUTTONS ARE ALWAYS THE HARDEST.

—Chapin in the St. Louis *Star.*

This cartoon was originally published in the *St. Louis Star* newspaper. Since 1807, only men had been legally allowed to vote in the United States. Suffragists, or activists for extending the right to vote to women, had been working for decades to overturn this. By the beginning of the 1900s, four states allowed women to vote at the state level. In 1918, President Woodrow Wilson began to support women's suffrage. In June of 1919, the legislature passed the Nineteenth Amendment, guaranteeing women the right to vote. However, thirty-six state legislatures had to ratify, or approve, the amendment before it could be official. This took until August of 1920.

3. During which of the following months is this cartoon most likely to have been published?

   A) June 1901

   B) August 1918

   C) June 1919

   D) March 1920

4. In the cartoon, what do the buttons represent?

   A) presidents who supported women's suffrage

   B) the number of amendments that needed to be passed

   C) states that are needed to ratify the Nineteenth Amendment

   D) steps in the process of finalizing a bill

Questions 5 – 7 refer to the following excerpt from *Common Sense*. Here, Paine describes the potential of America's military force:

Excerpt from *Common Sense*

BY THOMAS PAINE

No country on the globe is so happily situated, or so internally capable of raising a fleet as America. Tar, timber, iron, and cordage are her natural produce. We need go abroad for nothing. Whereas the Dutch, who make large profits by hiring out their ships of war to the Spaniards and Portuguese, are obliged to import most of their materials they use. We ought to view the building of a fleet as an article of commerce, it being the natural manufactory of this country. It is the best money we can lay out. A navy when finished is worth more than it cost. And is that nice point in national policy, in which commerce and protection are united. Let us build; if we want them not, we can sell; and by that means replace our paper currency with ready gold and silver...

In point of safety, ought we to be without a fleet? We are not the little people now, which we were sixty years ago; at that time we might have trusted our property in the streets, or fields rather; and slept securely without locks or bolts to our doors or windows. The case now is altered, and our methods of defense ought to improve with our increase of property. A common pirate, twelve months ago, might have come up the Delaware, and laid the city of Philadelphia under instant contribution, for what sum he pleased; and the same might have happened to other places. Nay, any daring fellow, in a brig of fourteen or sixteen guns might have robbed the whole continent, and carried off half a million of money. These are circumstances which demand our attention, and point out the necessity of naval protection.

Some, perhaps, will say, that after we have made it up with Britain, she will protect us. Can we be so unwise as to mean, that she shall keep a navy in our harbors for that purpose? Common sense will tell us, that the power which hath endeavored to subdue us, is of all others the most improper to defend us. Conquest may be affected under the pretense of friendship; and we after a long and brave resistance may be at last cheated into slavery. And if her ships are not to be admitted into our harbors, I would ask, how is she to protect us? A navy three or four thousand miles off can be of little use, and on sudden emergencies, none at all. Wherefore, if we must hereafter protect ourselves, why not do it for ourselves?

5. What does Thomas Paine indicate has changed over the past sixty years?

   A) Pirates are now more common.

   B) The American people now have much more property to protect.

   C) The relationship between America and Britain is now much friendlier.

   D) Guns have become more powerful, increasing the effectiveness of thieves.

6. The author most likely wanted America to produce a naval fleet to protect itself from

   A) Great Britain

   B) The Netherlands

   C) France

   D) Mexico

7. The author would most likely agree with which of the following points?

   A) America should maintain independence from Britain.

   B) Americans should attempt to return to a culture in which they could sleep without locking their doors.

   C) It's difficult to sell ships.

   D) It would be necessary to import ship-building materials to build the navy.

Questions 8 and 9 use information from the graph below:

AMERICAN IP INDEX

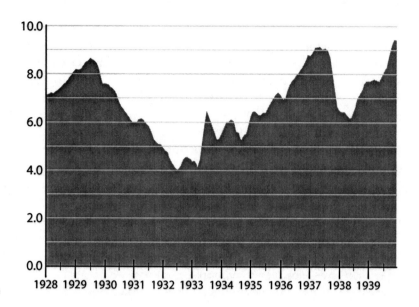

8. The longest period of decline in American manufacturing and mining occurred when?

   A) 1928 – 1929

   B) 1929 – 1932

   C) 1933 – 1935

   D) 1936 – 1938

9. Which of these most likely explains the drop in production in 1929?

   A) Demand for American-made goods dropped dramatically due to increases in foreign production.

   B) The United States Legislature introduced measures to increase domestic manufacturing.

   C) Panic in financial markets decreased the capital available to manufacturers.

   D) America's dominance in the automobile industry decreased its need to manufacture other goods.

Look at the map and answer question 10.

10. Based on the information in the map, which of the following conclusions is most likely?

    A) San Juan de Manapiare is one of the major centers of commerce in Venezuela.

    B) The majority of Venezuelans live in the northern part of the country.

    C) It's difficult to travel from Colombia to Venezuela by road.

    D) Colombia and Brazil frequently fight for control of territory in Venezuela.

Read the excerpt and answer question 11.

Article I, Section 3 of the United States Constitution:

The Senate of the United States shall be composed of two Senators from each State, chosen by the Legislature thereof for six Years; and each Senator shall have one Vote.

Immediately after they shall be assembled in Consequence of the first Election, they shall be divided as equally as may be into three Classes. The Seats of the Senators of the first Class shall be vacated at the Expiration of the second Year, of the second Class at the Expiration of the fourth Year, and of the third Class at the Expiration of the sixth Year, so that one third may be chosen every second Year; and if Vacancies happen by Resignation, or otherwise, during the Recess of the Legislature of any State, the Executive thereof may make temporary Appointments until the next Meeting of the Legislature, which shall then fill such Vacancies.

No Person shall be a Senator who shall not have attained to the Age of thirty Years, and been nine Years a Citizen of the United States, and who shall not, when elected, be an Inhabitant of that State for which he shall be chosen.

The Vice President of the United States shall be President of the Senate, but shall have no Vote, unless they are equally divided.

The Senate shall choose their other Officers, and also a President pro tempore, in the Absence of the Vice President, or when he shall exercise the Office of President of the United States.

The Senate shall have the sole Power to try all Impeachments. When sitting for that Purpose, they shall be on Oath or Affirmation. When the President of the United States is tried, the Chief Justice shall preside: And no Person shall be convicted without the Concurrence of two thirds of the Members present.

Judgment in Cases of Impeachment shall not extend further than to removal from Office, and disqualification to hold and enjoy any Office of honor, Trust or Profit under the United States: but the Party convicted shall nevertheless be liable and subject to Indictment, Trial, Judgment and Punishment, according to Law.

11. Of the following people, who would not be eligible to serve in the Senate today based on the information given?

    A) a thirty-year-old man

    B) a forty-two-year-old woman

    C) a person elected to serve as a senator for a state in which he does not live

    D) a person who obtained U.S. citizenship in the 1980s

Read the excerpt and answer questions 12 and 13.

Article I, Section 3 of the United States Constitution

The Senate shall have the sole power to try all impeachments. When sitting for that purpose, they shall be on oath or affirmation. When the President of the United States is tried, the Chief Justice shall preside: and no person shall be convicted without the concurrence of two thirds of the members present.

12. This section of the Constitution is an example of which principle?

    A) proportional representation

    B) freedom of speech

    C) the separation of church and state

    D) separation of powers

13. Which of the following best describes the vice president's role in the Senate?

    A) The vice president acts as a member of the Senate.

    B) The vice president presides over Senate sessions but is never allowed to vote.

    C) The vice president presides over the Senate during impeachment trials.

    D) The vice president presides over Senate sessions and breaks ties in Senate votes.

Read the excerpt and answer questions 14 and 15.

In 1913, the United States created the Federal Reserve System, partially in response to financial panics in the years prior. The Federal Reserve System is tasked with using monetary policy to help the United States weather economic fluctuations, maintain employment rates, and keep inflation to a predictable rate. While high-ranking members of the Federal Reserve Board are appointed by the president and confirmed by the Senate, the Federal Reserve is able to make decisions about monetary policy without approval by the branches of government.

14. Which of the following outcomes is prevented by giving the Federal Reserve System decision-making power independent of the branches of government?

    A) the Federal Reserve System using monetary policy to prevent high inflation

    B) the president of the United States appointing the chair of the Federal Reserve System

    C) the Senate influencing economic outcomes by setting monetary policy

    D) the Federal Reserve System preventing financial panics

15. Which of the following is not a situation in which the Federal Reserve System would be expected to act?

A) Parts of the country are experiencing dangerously high inflation rates.

B) A downturn in manufacturing causes an unexpected spike in unemployment.

C) A financial panic causes banks to close.

D) The Senate requests that funding for the military be increased.

Look at the chart and answer questions 16 – 18.

Significant inventions in textile production during the Industrial Revolution

YEAR	INVENTION	EFFECT ON PRODUCTIVITY
1733	**FLYING SHUTTLE**: A device that allows one worker to weave across a wide loom quickly.	This tool was estimated to have doubled the productivity of one weaver.
1764	**SPINNING JENNY**: A device that allows one worker to produce several spools of yarn at one time, using a frame operated by a wheel.	At first, workers could spin eight spools of yarn at once rather than one. As the technology improved, this increased to as many as 120 spools at once.
1764	**WATER FRAME**: Another device used for spinning multiple spools of thread at once, the water frame used power sufficient to produce high-quality threads.	With the introduction of the water frame, both the warp and the weft threads needed for making cotton cloth could now be produced by fully mechanized means.
1779	**SPINNING MULE**: This combined the technologies of the spinning jenny and the water frame, allowing higher-quality threads to be produced.	The cloth produced with the spinning mule was able to compete with higher-quality, more costly handmade fabrics.

16. Based on the chart, what was the main reason these inventions were introduced into textile production?

A) to increase the productivity of workers

B) to decrease the need to hire workers

C) to ease the burden on tired workers

D) to allow more workers to open their own textile factories

17. Each of these devices was invented in Great Britain. Which of the following is a likely effect these inventions had on that nation's economy?

A) British manufacturers profited by producing low-cost textiles that they sold overseas.

B) British manufacturers profited by producing textiles that were not affordable in other countries.

C) British manufacturers lost money by producing low-quality textiles that did not sell well.

D) British manufacturers profited by producing high-quality, high-cost textiles.

18. The inventions discussed in the chart explain which shifts in the lives of textile workers during the 1700s?

A) They faced more dangerous tasks and earned lower wages.

B) They became more productive and learned to use new machinery.

C) They earned higher wages but faced more dangerous conditions.

D) Their working conditions improved as they unionized.

Look at the poster and answer questions 19 and 20.

During World War I, food shortages became a problem in the United States and many other countries, as those who worked in agriculture enlisted in military service and food production regions in Europe became battlegrounds. To address food shortages domestically, the government encouraged citizens to plant their own vegetables at home or in public spaces such as parks.

Victory gardens came to the forefront again when the forced internment of over 100,000 Japanese Americans drastically reduced the agricultural capacity of the American West.

19. What was the purpose of the poster shown previously?

   A) to promote the idea of victory gardens

   B) to teach people how to plant a victory garden

   C) to encourage people to enlist in military service.

   D) to encourage healthy eating habits

20. During which period were Japanese Americans forced into internment camps?

   A) before World War I

   B) during World War I

   C) during the period between World War I and World War II

   D) during World War II

Look at the cartoon below and answer questions 21 and 22.

IN THE RUBBER COILS.

Scene – The Congo "Free" State.

In 1885, King Leopold of Belgium declared the Congo, the largest state in the African continent, to be his colony: the Congo Free State. The territory remained under his control until 1908, and during that time, Leopold used his power to brutally extract natural resources, including rubber, ivory, and mined minerals.

21. The snake in the cartoon above is depicting whom or what?

    A)   the Belgian government

    B)   King Leopold

    C)   the rubber companies

    D)   public outrage

$\longrightarrow$
CONTINUE

22. The artist who drew this cartoon likely believed that

    A) the Congolese people were suffering under King Leopold.

    B) people should boycott the rubber trade.

    C) the Congo Free State should not belong to Belgium.

    D) the Republic of the Congo could benefit economically from producing rubber.

Look at the chart below and answer questions 23 – 25.

Acts of Congress

YEAR	ACT	DESCRIPTION
1789	United States Constitution, Article III	Establishes that all crimes, with the exception of impeachment cases, must be tried by a jury in the state in which they were committed.
1791	Sixth Amendment of the Constitution (Bill of Rights)	Requires that each individual member of a jury be unbiased, or without preconceptions, toward the defendant. To ensure that bias does not exist, both the prosecution and the defense sides of a trial have the chance to interview prospective jurors and eliminate those whom they find to have a bias.
1968	Jury Selection and Service Act	A comprehensive reform of the jury selection process, this act made every district court in the U.S. compile names of potential jurors from voter registration lists or voting records. These lists could be supplemented by other means if they did not accurately reflect the demographics (age, race, gender) of the community.

23. Which of the following rights of those on trial was guaranteed by the Jury Selection and Service Act?

    A) The trial must occur in the state in which the crime was committed.

    B) The trial jury must be unbiased.

    C) The jury must be composed such that it reflects the demographics of the community.

    D) The defense has the opportunity to eliminate jurors whom they find to be biased before the trial begins.

24. The United States Declaration of Independence, adopted in 1776, denounced the British monarchy for often denying its subjects a trial by jury for accused crimes. Which of the following seeks to address this?

    A) Article III of the Constitution

    B) the Sixth Amendment of the Constitution (in the Bill of Rights)

    C) the Jury Selection and Service Act

    D) none of the above

25. Which of these best explains why the Jury Selection and Service Act was passed?

    A) to ensure that only capable individuals are assigned to juries

    B) to ensure that jurors do not allow their own prejudices to sway their decisions

    C) to ensure that only individuals who vote are able to serve on juries

    D) to ensure that minorities are not excluded from juries

Read the letters below and answer questions 26 and 27.

Letter 1	Letter 2
Dear Editor, I am concerned about the proposed free-trade agreement between the United States and the countries of the European Union. The North American Free Trade Agreement, between the United States, Canada, and Mexico, makes more sense to me because we are all neighbors and we do not produce the same types of goods, so there is less competition and more reason to trade. However in Germany for example, auto manufacturing is an important industry. If we remove the taxes from imported cars, fewer people will buy American-made cars because German cars will become cheaper than they are now. This will hurt our domestic industries. My son works in an auto plant, and if demand for American cars goes down, he could lose his job.	Dear Editor, I am writing because I manage a small clothing business, and a free-trade agreement between the US and the EU would positively impact my bottom line. I design swimsuits and other garments, which are mostly manufactured in the Czech Republic due to its strong garment-manufacturing resources. When I ship the raw materials there and then when my vendors ship the finished products back to me, we are taxed twice, raising the prices of my clothes. Then, through online sales, we ship some clothes to countries in the EU—and are taxed again. Eliminating this triple tax means that my clothes will ultimately be cheaper for everyone. This must be true for many businesses, so a free-trade agreement would mean cheaper consumer goods for all.

26. The author of Letter 1 compares the proposed free-trade agreement with what?

    A) the American auto industry

    B) the global garment market

    C) the North American Free Trade Agreement

    D) the European Union

27. Which of the following accurately describes the production chain that the author of Letter 2 uses in his or her argument?

    A) Swimsuits are designed and manufactured in the Czech Republic and then shipped to the United States, where they are purchased and shipped to customers in countries in the European Union.

    B) Swimsuits are designed in the United States, manufactured in the European Union, and then shipped back to the United States, where they are sold or shipped to customers in the European Union.

    C) Swimsuits are designed in the United States, manufactured in the European Union, and then sold to customers in the European Union.

    D) Swimsuits are designed and manufactured in the United States, then shipped to customers in the Czech Republic and other countries in the European Union.

→

CONTINUE

Look at the chart and answer questions 28 and 29.

AUGUST 6, 1945	The United States bombs the Japanese cities Hiroshima and Nagasaki with atomic weapons during World War II.
MARCH 5, 1946	British Prime Minister Winston Churchill gives his famous speech warning of the "Iron Curtain" of communism falling across Europe, separating the Soviet Union and its satellites from the rest of Europe.
MARCH 12, 1946	U.S. President Harry Truman announces that the U.S. will give monetary aid to Greece and Turkey to prevent them from falling under Soviet control.
JUNE 5, 1947	U.S. Secretary of State George Marshall announces that the U.S. will give aid to all war-ravaged countries in Western Europe to prevent the spread of Soviet communism.

28. What event must have happened between August 6, 1945, and March 5, 1946?

    A)   The United States tested its first atomic bomb.

    B)   The Marshall Plan was announced.

    C)   The Soviet Union began to exert influence over its satellite countries.

    D)   World War II ended.

29. During the 1940s, what was the primary diplomatic means by which the United States worked to contain communism?

    A)   constructing the Iron Curtain

    B)   giving aid to other countries

    C)   testing nuclear weapons

    D)   declaring war on the Soviet Union

Read the excerpt and answer questions 30 and 31.

The World Bank was established in 1944 during the Bretton Woods Conference concerning international financial stability. The World Bank is intended to combat global poverty by assisting developing countries with loans for programs to benefit their citizens. In 1994 the World Bank, together with the International Monetary Fund, began a debt-relief program to help thirty-nine countries classified as heavily indebted and poor.

Critics of the World Bank say that its aid comes with overly stringent requirements: for example, to qualify for a World Bank loan, many countries in sub-Saharan Africa have undergone structural adjustment policies. These policies require countries' state-owned resources to be sold to private companies and their expensive government-run social programs to be cut. While it could be argued that structural adjustment policies are intended to be beneficial by stimulating economic growth, when they are implemented too quickly or without proper support they can actually trigger economic depressions instead.

30. What is the stated purpose of the World Bank?

    A)   to implement structural adjustment policies

    B)   to cancel out the debt of developing countries

    C)   to combat global poverty

    D)   to sell state-owned resources to private companies

31. Which of the following actions of the World Bank would a critic of the World Bank view as a harmful policy?

   A) loaning 60 million dollars to Rwanda to improve access to electricity

   B) giving Nicaragua a structural adjustment credit for selling state-owned assets to foreign investors

   C) loaning money to Lebanon for the purpose of hiring unemployed young people in government roles

   D) funding a program to enforce wastewater treatment regulations in industrialized areas of Vietnam

Read the excerpt and answer questions 32 – 35.

To ensure the peaceful development of nations, free from coercion, the United States has taken a leading part in establishing the United Nations. The United Nations is designed to make possible lasting freedom and independence for all its members. We shall not realize our objectives, however, unless we are willing to help free peoples to maintain their free institutions and their national integrity against aggressive movements that seek to impose upon them totalitarian regimes. This is no more than a frank recognition that totalitarian regimes imposed on free peoples, by direct or indirect aggression, undermine the foundations of international peace and hence the security of the United States.

The peoples of a number of countries of the world have recently had totalitarian regimes forced upon them against their will. The Government of the United States has made frequent protests against coercion and intimidation, in violation of the Yalta agreement, in Poland, Rumania, and Bulgaria. I must also state that in a number of other countries there have been similar developments.

At the present moment in world history nearly every nation must choose between alternative ways of life. The choice is too often not a free one.

One way of life is based upon the will of the majority, and is distinguished by free institutions, representative government, free elections, guarantees of individual liberty, freedom of speech and religion, and freedom from political oppression.

The second way of life is based upon the will of a minority forcibly imposed upon the majority. It relies upon terror and oppression, a controlled press and radio; fixed elections, and the suppression of personal freedoms.

I believe that it must be the policy of the United States to support free peoples who are resisting attempted subjugation by armed minorities or by outside pressures.

80th Cong. 171 (1947)(Statement of Harry Truman, President of the United States) March 12, 1947 (Truman Doctrine)

32. How does Truman differentiate between the two ways of life he discusses in his speech?

   A) He describes one as better than the other.

   B) He describes one as based on free institutions, speech, elections, religion, but politically oppressive, while the other is based on oppression, suppressed radio, press, and personal freedoms, but with some political freedoms.

   C) He describes one free from political oppression and the other with only limited political freedoms.

   D) He describes one as based on free institutions, speech, elections, religion, and freedom from political oppression, while the other is based on oppression, rigged elections, and suppressed radio, press, and personal freedoms.

CONTINUE

33. Read this sentence from the text.

This is no more than a frank recognition that totalitarian regimes imposed on free peoples, by direct or indirect aggression, undermine the foundations of international peace and hence the security of the United States.

In the context of the excerpt, how is this idea comparable with the Bush doctrine of preemption?

A) It argues that communism is a threat to U.S. security.

B) It states that the U.S. must protect its national sovereignty.

C) It argues that the U.S. must assist countries before they are taken over by totalitarian forces; otherwise, national security is at risk.

D) It argues that the U.S. must assist countries after they are taken over by totalitarian forces; otherwise, national security is at risk.

34. Read this excerpt from the text.

The peoples of a number of countries of the world have recently had totalitarian regimes forced upon them against their will. The Government of the United States has made frequent protests against coercion and intimidation, in violation of the Yalta agreement, in Poland, Rumania, and Bulgaria. I must also state that in a number of other countries there have been similar developments.

To what historical developments is Truman referring?

A) the occupation of the Sudetenland and Poland, among other European countries, by Hitler

B) the occupation of several Eastern European countries by Stalin

C) the construction of the Berlin Wall and the occupation of Poland, Romania, and Bulgaria by the U.S.S.R.

D) the construction of the Iron Curtain

35. When discussing the "two ways of life," what is Truman describing?

A) the differences between communism and democratic capitalism—that is, between the U.S. and the U.S.S.R.

B) the differences between communism and democratic totalitarianism—that is, between the U.S.S.R. and the European Union

C) the differences between communism and fascism—that is, between the U.S.S.R. and Nazi Germany

D) the differences between democratic capitalism and fascism—that is, between the U.S. and the U.S.S.R.

Read the excerpt and answer questions 36 and 37.

It's not true that the United States feels any land hunger or entertains any projects as regards the other nations of the Western Hemisphere save such as are for their welfare. All that this country desires is to see the neighboring countries stable, orderly, and prosperous. Any country whose people conduct themselves well can count upon our hearty friendship. If a nation shows that it knows how to act with reasonable efficiency and decency in social and political matters, if it keeps order and pays its obligations, it need fear no interference from the United States. Chronic wrongdoing, or an impotence which results in a general loosening of the ties of civilized society, may in America, as elsewhere, ultimately require intervention by some civilized nation, and in the Western Hemisphere the adherence of the United States to the Monroe

Doctrine may force the United States, however reluctantly, in flagrant cases of such wrongdoing or impotence, to the exercise of an international police power.

Theodore Roosevelt's Annual Message to Congress, December 6, 1904 (Roosevelt Corollary to the Monroe Doctrine)

36. What is Roosevelt saying about U.S. intentions in the Western Hemisphere?

A) The United States will not intervene in domestic matters in Latin American countries.

B) The United States will only intervene in domestic matters in Latin American countries upon request.

C) The United States will intervene in Latin American countries when it sees fit.

D) The United States will intervene in Latin American countries when it sees fit and may use force.

37. According to the Monroe Doctrine, the United States would view European interference in Latin America as a sign of aggression, consolidating U.S. influence in that region. What is different about the Roosevelt Corollary to the Monroe Doctrine?

A) It stationed U.S. troops throughout Latin America.

B) It strengthened commercial ties between the United States and Latin American countries.

C) It limited diplomatic relations between Europe and Latin America.

D) It provided for U.S. military intervention in Latin America.

Read the excerpt and answer questions 38–41.

Niger is a landlocked, sub-Saharan nation, whose economy centers on subsistence crops, livestock, and some of the world's largest uranium deposits. Agriculture contributes nearly 40% of GDP and provides livelihood for most of the population. The UN ranked Niger as the least developed country in the world in 2014 due to multiple factors such as food insecurity, lack of industry, high population growth, a weak educational sector, and few prospects for work outside of subsistence farming and herding. Since 2011 public debt has increased in part from a large loan financing a new uranium mine. The government relies on foreign donor resources for a large portion of its fiscal budget. The economy in recent years has been hurt by terrorist activity and kidnappings near its uranium mines and instability in Mali, and concerns about security have boosted fiscal spending on defense. Future growth may be sustained by exploitation of oil, gold, coal, and other mineral resources. Niger has sizable reserves of oil and oil production. Food insecurity and drought remain perennial problems for Niger, and the government plans to invest more in the agriculture sector, most notably irrigation. The mining sector may be affected by the government's attempt to renegotiate extraction rights contracts to increase royalty rates and reduce tax exemptions. Despite Niger's three-year $121 million IMF Extended Credit Facility agreement for years 2012-2015, formal private sector investment needed for economic diversification and growth remains a challenge, given the country's limited domestic markets, access to credit, and competitiveness.

Reprinted from the CIA World Factbook,
https://www.ciA)gov/library/publications/the-world-factbook/geos/ng.html

38. Given the information above, what is likely true about Niger?

A) Rates of infant and child mortality are low.

B) Rates of infant and child mortality are high.

C) It's unlikely that Niger was formerly a European colony.

D) Cities are growing in Niger.

39. Reasons for Niger's status as an LDC include all the following EXCEPT:

   A) its drought-prone geography and climate

   B) low levels of industrialization

   C) Niger's amount of mineral resources

   D) social insecurity

40. What would a demographer working in Niger likely study?

   A) how changes in the land and climate affect the movements of farmers and herders

   B) the push-and-pull factors driving Nigeriens into Niger's growing cities

   C) government monetary and debt policies

   D) the growing threats of kidnapping and violence near uranium mines

41. According to the reading, what is currently an important source of revenue for Niger?

   A) cattle

   B) uranium

   C) agriculture

   D) defense

Read the excerpt and answer questions 42 – 44.

Article 41

The Security Council may decide what measures not involving the use of armed force are to be employed to give effect to its decisions, and it may call upon the Members of the United Nations to apply such measures. These may include complete or partial interruption of economic relations and of rail, sea, air, postal, telegraphic, radio, and other means of communication, and the severance of diplomatic relations.

Article 42

Should the Security Council consider that measures provided for in Article 41 would be inadequate or have proved to be inadequate, it may take such action by air, sea or land forces as may be necessary to maintain or restore international peace and security. Such action may include demonstrations, blockade, and other operations by air, sea, or land forces of Members of the United Nations.

United Nations, Charter of the United Nations, 24 October 1945, 1 UNTS XVI, Chapter VII

42. According to Article 42, what action can the Security Council take to maintain international peace and security?

   A) It may impose embargoes on countries.

   B) It may force the General Assembly to take military action against countries.

   C) It may cut diplomatic relations with countries.

   D) It may take military action against countries.

43. What is the difference between the Security Council and the League of Nations?

   A) The Security Council can take military action to preserve international peace and security.

   B) The Security Council can compel countries to sever diplomatic ties to preserve international peace and security.

   C) The Security Council can take control of national military forces.

   D) The Security Council cannot take military action.

44. Read this sentence from the text.

These may include complete or partial interruption of economic relations and of rail, sea, air, postal, telegraphic, radio, and other means of communication, and the severance of diplomatic relations.

By taking these steps, the Security Council would likely be aiming for all the following outcomes EXCEPT:

A) to make the people suffer

B) to make the country change its policy

C) to encourage the country to negotiate

D) to avoid international military action

Read the excerpt and answer the questions that follow.

Four score and seven years ago our fathers brought forth, upon this continent, a new nation, conceived in liberty, and dedicated to the proposition that "all men are created equal."

Now we are engaged in a great civil war, testing whether that nation, or any nation so conceived, and so dedicated, can long endure.

Abraham Lincoln, the Gettysburg Address

45. Read this sentence from the passage.

Four score and seven years ago our fathers brought forth, upon this continent, a new nation, conceived in liberty, and dedicated to the proposition that "all men are created equal."

What was President Lincoln referring to here?

A) the Civil War

B) the American Revolution

C) the writing of the Constitution

D) the creation of the Bill of Rights

46. What statement would the author of this passage agree with?

A) The outcome of the Civil War would only impact the United States.

B) The Civil War would be the final battle for American independence.

C) The outcome of the Civil War would impact the future of any democracy based on equality.

D) The Civil War was a war for states' rights.

47. Why did President Lincoln speak at Gettysburg?

A) It was the site of a major Revolutionary War battle.

B) It was the site of an important debate about states' rights.

C) It was the site of a major Civil War battle.

D) It was the site of the signing of the Declaration of Independence.

ANSWER KEY

Social Studies

1. C)		**13.** D)		**25.** D)		**37.** D)
2. A)		**14.** C)		**26.** C)		**38.** B)
3. D)		**15.** D)		**27.** B)		**39.** C)
4. C)		**16.** A)		**28.** C)		**40.** A)
5. B)		**17.** A)		**29.** B)		**41.** B)
6. A)		**18.** B)		**30.** C)		**42.** D)
7. A)		**19.** A)		**31.** B)		**43.** A)
8. B)		**20.** D)		**32.** D)		**44.** A)
9. C)		**21.** B)		**33.** C)		**45.** B)
10. B)		**22.** A)		**34.** B)		**46.** C)
11. C)		**23.** C)		**35.** A)		**47.** C)
12. D)		**24.** A)		**36.** D)		